O my Lord,
O primeval Philosopher,
Maintainer of the universe,
O regulating Principle,
Destination of the pure devotees,
Well-wisher of the progenitors of mankind,
please remove the effulgence of Your transcendental rays,
so that I can see Your Form of Bliss.
You are the eternal Supreme Personality of Godhead,
like unto the sun, as am I.

[Mantra Sixteen, p.91]

His Divine Grace

A.C. Bhaktivedanta Swami Prabhupāda

Founder-Ācārya of the International Society for Krishna Consciousness

"The Vedas are considered to be the mother and Brahmā is called the grandfather, the forefather, because he was first to be instructed in the Vedic knowledge. In the beginning the first living creature was Brahmā." **p. 4**

"Lord Nṛsiṁha appeared from within the pillar not at the order of the atheist king, but by the wish of the devotee, Prahlāda. An atheist cannot order the Lord to appear, but to show mercy to His devotee the Lord can appear anywhere and everywhere." **p. 33**

"By worshipping the *Arcā-vigraha* of the Lord, one can at once approach the Lord, Who accepts the service of the devotee by His omnipotent energy without any reproach." **p. 45**

“Beyond these two there is the Kāraṇodaka-śāyī Viṣṇu lying in the causal ocean. He is the Creator of all the Universes.” **p. 88**

"...it can be summarized in short that by His one Plenary portion—the all-pervading *Paramātman*—He maintains the complete material cosmic creation." **p. 86-95**

"The Personality of Godhead… played with the cowherd boys who had achieved that position after a huge accumulation of pious deeds." **p. 87-93**

"Mahārāj Parīkṣit's question was, 'What is the duty of every man, specifically at the time of death?' The answer by Goswāmī Śukadeva was that everyone who is desireous of being free from all anxieties should always hear about and glorify the Personality of Godhead..." **p. 102-103**

श्री ईशोपनिषद्

ŚRĪ ĪŚOPANIṢAD

BOOKS by

His Divine Grace

A.C. Bhaktivedanta Swami Prabhupāda

published by *Krishna Books Inc*

Bhagavad-gītā As It Is
Śrīmad Bhāgavatam (30 volume set)
Śrī Caitanya-caritāmṛta (17 volume set)
Kṛṣṇa, the Supreme Personality of Godhead
Teachings of Lord Chaitanya
Teachings of Queen Kuntī
Śrī Īśopaniṣad
The Nectar of Devotion
The Science of Self-Realization
Rāja-vidyā: The King of Knowledge
Easy Journey to Other Planets
Kṛṣṇa, the Reservoir of Pleasure
The Perfection of Yoga
Beyond Birth and Death
On Chanting Hare Kṛṣṇa
Life Comes From Life
The Path of Perfection
Perfect Questions, Perfect Answers
Search for Liberation

Śrī Īśopaniṣad

The knowledge that brings one nearer to the Supreme Personality of Godhead, Kṛṣṇa.

with original Sanskrit text,
Roman transliteration,
English equivalents, translation
and elaborate purports

His Divine Grace
A.C. Bhaktivedanta Swami Prabhupāda

Founder-Ācārya of the International Society for Krishna Consciousness

Śrī Īśopaniṣad

Contains the original text found in the first edition published by ISKCON Books in 1969

Krishna Books Inc is licensed by the *Bhaktivedanta Book Trust* to print and publish the literary works of

His Divine Grace
A. C. Bhaktivedanta Swami Prabhupāda

Readers interested in obtaining other titles by the author may contact Krishna Books Inc:

www.krishnabooks.org

or email: info@krishnabooks.org

Library of Congress Catalog Card Number: 78-102853

1969 English Edition ISBN: 978-1-60293-001-8

KBI Reprint 2016

Printed and bound by Thomson Press (India) Ltd.

TABLE OF CONTENTS

INTRODUCTION

(Teachings of the Vedas)

[Delivered as a lecture by His Divine Grace A.C. Bhaktivedānta Swāmī Prabhupāda on October 6, 1969, at Conway Hall, London, England.]

Ladies and gentlemen, today's subject matter is the teachings of the *Vedas*. What are the *Vedas*? The Sanskrit verbal root of *Veda* can be interpreted variously, but the purpose is finally one. *Veda* means knowledge. Any knowledge you accept is *Veda*, for the teachings of the *Vedas* are the original knowledge. In the conditioned state, our knowledge is subjected to so many deficiencies. The difference between a conditioned soul and a liberated soul is that the conditioned soul has four kinds of defects. The first defect is that he must commit mistakes. For example, in our country, Mahātmā Gandhi was considered to be a very great personality, but he committed many mistakes. Even at the last stage of his life, his assistant warned, "Mahātmā Gandhi, don't go to the New Delhi meeting. I have some friends and I have heard there is danger." But he did not hear. He persisted on going and was killed. Even great personalities like Mahātmā Gandhi, President Kennedy—there are so many of them—make mistakes. To err is human. This is one defect of the conditioned soul.

Another defect: to be illusioned. Illusion means to accept something which is not: *māyā*. *Māyā* means what is not. Everyone is accepting the body as the self. If I ask you what you are, you will say, "I am Mr. John; I am a rich man; I am this, I am that." All these are bodily identifications. But you are not this body. This is illusion.

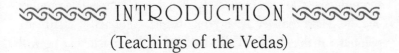

The third defect is the cheating propensity. Everyone has the propensity to cheat others. Although a person is fool number one, he poses himself as very intelligent. Although it is already pointed out that he is in illusion and makes mistakes, he will theorize: "I think this is this, this is this." But he does not even know his own position. He writes books of philosophy, although he is defective. That is his disease. That is cheating.

Lastly, our senses are imperfect. We are very proud of our eyes. Often, someone will challenge, "Can you show me God?" But do you have the eyes to see God? You will never see if you haven't the eyes. If immediately the room becomes dark, you cannot even see your hands. So what power do you have to see? We cannot, therefore, expect knowledge *(Vedas)* with these imperfect senses. With all these deficiencies, in conditioned life, we cannot give perfect knowledge to anyone. Nor are we ourselves perfect. Therefore we accept the *Vedas* as they are.

You may call the *Vedas* Hindu, but Hindu is a foreign name. We are not Hindus. Our real identification is *varṇāśrama. Varṇāśrama* denotes the followers of the *Vedas,* those who accept the human society in eight divisions of *varṇa* and *āśrama*. There are four divisions of society and four divisions of spiritual life. This is called *varṇāśrama*. It is stated in the *Bhagavad-gītā,* "These divisions are there everywhere, because they are created by God." The divisions of society are *brāhmaṇa, kṣatriya, vaiśya, śūdra. Brāhmaṇa* refers to the very intelligent class of men, those who know what is *Brahman*. Similarly, the *kṣatriyas,* the administrator group, are the next intelligent class of men. Then the *vaiśyas,* the mercantile group. These natural classifications are found everywhere. This is the Vedic principle, and we accept it. Vedic principles are accepted as axiomatic truth, for there cannot be any mistake. That is acceptance. For instance, in India, cow dung is accepted as pure, and yet cow dung is the stool of an animal. In one place you'll find the Vedic injunction that if you touch stool, you have to take a bath immediately. But in another place it is said that the stool of a cow is pure. If you smear cow dung in an impure place that place becomes pure. With our ordinary sense we can argue, "This is contradictory." Actually, it is contradictory from the ordinary point of view, but it is not false. It is fact. In Calcutta, a very prominent scientist and doctor analyzed cow dung and found that it contains all antiseptic properties.

In India if one person tells another, "You must do this," the other party may say, "What do you mean? Is this a Vedic injunction that I have to follow you without any argument?" Vedic injunctions cannot be interpreted. But ultimately, if you carefully study why these injunctions are there, you will find that they are all correct.

The *Vedas* are not compilations of human knowledge. Vedic knowledge comes from the Spiritual World, from Lord Kṛṣṇa. Another name for the *Vedas* is *śruti*. *Śruti* refers to that knowledge which is acquired by hearing. It is not experimental knowledge. *Śruti* is considered to be like a mother. We take so much knowledge from our mother. For example, if you want to know who your father is, who can answer you? Your mother. If the mother says, "Here is your father," you have to accept it. It is not possible to experiment to find out whether he is your father. Similarly, if you want to know something beyond your experience, beyond your experimental knowledge, beyond the activities of the senses, then you have to accept *Vedas*. There is no question of experimenting. It has already been experimented. It is already settled. The version of the mother, for instance, has to be accepted as truth. There is no other way.

The *Vedas* are considered to be the mother and Brahmā is called the grandfather, the forefather, because he was the first to be instructed in the Vedic knowledge. In the beginning the first living creature was Brahmā. He received this Vedic knowledge and imparted it to Nārada and other disciples and sons, and they also distributed it to their disciples. In this way, the Vedic knowledge comes down by disciplic succession. It is also confirmed in the *Bhagavad-gītā,* that Vedic knowledge is understood in this way. If you make experimental endeavor, you come to the same conclusion, but just to save time you should accept. If you want to know who your father is and if you accept your mother as authority, then whatever she says can be accepted without argument. There are three kinds of evidences: *pratyakṣa, anumāṇa* and *śabda. Pratyakṣa* means direct. Direct evidence is not so good because our senses are not perfect. We are seeing the sun daily, and it appears to us just like a small disc, but it is actually far, far larger than many planets. Of what value is this seeing? Therefore we have to read books, then we can understand about the sun. So direct experience is not perfect. Then there is inductive knowledge: "It may be like this," hypothesis. For instance, Darwin's theory says it may be like this, it may be like that, but that is not science. That is a suggestion, and it is also not perfect. But if you receive the knowledge from the authoritative sources, that is perfect. If you receive a program guide from the radio station authorities, you accept it. You don't deny it; you don't have to make an experiment because it is received from the authoritative sources.

Vedic knowledge is called *śabda-pramāṇa.* Another name is *śruti. Śruti* means that this knowledge has to be received simply by aural reception. The *Vedas* instruct that in order to understand transcendental knowledge we have to hear from the authority. Transcendental knowledge is knowledge from beyond this universe. Within this universe is material knowledge, and beyond this universe is transcendental knowledge. We cannot even go to the end of the universe, so how can we go to the Spiritual World? Thus to acquire full knowledge is impossible.

There is a Spiritual Sky. There is another nature that is beyond manifestation and non-manifestation. But how will you know that there is a sky where the planets and inhabitants are eternal? All this knowledge is there, but how will you make experiments? It is not possible. Therefore you have to take the assistance of the *Vedas*. This is called Vedic knowledge. In our Kṛṣṇa Consciousness Movement, we are accepting knowledge from the highest authority, Kṛṣṇa. Kṛṣṇa is accepted as the highest authority by all classes of men. I am speaking first of the two classes of transcendentalists. One class of transcendentalist is called impersonalist, *Māyā-vādī*. They are generally known as Vedāntists, led by Śaṅkarācārya. And there is another class of transcendentalist, called Vaiṣṇavas, like Rāmānujācārya, Madhvācārya, Viṣṇusvāmī. Both the Śaṅkara-sampradāya and the Vaiṣṇava-sampradāya have accepted Kṛṣṇa as the Supreme Personality of Godhead. Śaṅkarācārya is supposed to be an impersonalist who preached impersonalism, impersonal *Brahman*, but it is a fact that he is a covered personalist. In his commentary on the *Bhagavad-gītā* he wrote: "Nārāyana, the Supreme Personality of Godhead, is beyond this cosmic manifestation." And then again he confirms, "That Supreme Personality of Godhead, Nārāyana, is Kṛṣṇa. He has come as the Son of Devakī and Vasudeva." He has particularly mentioned the names of His father and mother. So Kṛṣṇa is accepted as the Supreme Personality of Godhead by all transcendentalists. There is no doubt about it. Our source of knowledge in Kṛṣṇa Consciousness is directly from Kṛṣṇa, *Bhagavad-gītā*. We have published *Bhagavad Gītā As It Is*, because we accept Kṛṣṇa as He is speaking without any interpretation. That is Vedic knowledge. Since the Vedic knowledge is pure, we accept it. Whatever Kṛṣṇa says, we accept. This is Kṛṣṇa Consciousness. That saves much time. If you accept the right authority or the source of knowledge, then you save much time. For example, there are two systems of knowledge in the material world, inductive and deductive. From deductive, you accept that man is mortal. Your father says man is mortal, your sister says man is mortal, everyone says man is mortal—but you do not experiment. You accept it as fact that man is mortal. If you want to research to find out whether man is mortal, you have to study each and every man, and you may come to think that there may be some man who is not dying, but you have not seen him yet. So in this way your researching will never be finished. This process is called in Sanskrit, *āroha*, the ascending process. If you want to attain knowledge by any personal endeavor, by exercising your imperfect senses, you will never come to the right conclusions. That is not possible.

There is a statement in *Brahma-saṁhitā:* Just ride on the airplane which runs at the speed of mind. Our material airplanes can run 2,000 miles per hour, but what is the speed of mind? You are sitting at home, you immediately think of India, say 10,000 miles away, and at once it is in your home. Your mind has gone there. The mind-speed is so swift. Therefore it is stated, "If you travel at this speed for millions of years, you'll find that the Spiritual Sky is unlimited. It is not possible even to approach it. Therefore, the Vedic injunction is that one must approach—the word "compulsory" is used—a bona fide spiritual master, a *guru*. And what is the qualification of a spiritual master? He has rightly heard the Vedic message from the right source. Otherwise he is not bona fide. He must practically be firmly established in *Brahman*. These are the two qualities. This Kṛṣṇa Consciousness movement is completely authorized from Vedic principles. In the *Bhagavad-gītā* Kṛṣṇa says, "The actual aim of Vedic research is to find out Kṛṣṇa." In the *Brahma-saṁhitā* it is also stated, "Kṛṣṇa, Govinda, has innumerable Forms, but they are all one." They are not like our forms, which are fallible. His Form is infallible. My form has a beginning, but His Form has no beginning. It is *ananta*. And His Form—so many multiforms—has no end. My form is sitting here and not in my apartment. You are sitting there and not in your apartment. But Kṛṣṇa can be anywhere at one time. He can sit down in Goloka Vṛndāvana and at the same time He is everywhere, all-pervading. He is Original, the Oldest, but whenever you look at a picture of Kṛṣṇa you'll find a young Boy of 15-20 years old. You will never find an old man. You have seen pictures of Kṛṣṇa as a charioteer from the *Bhagavad-gītā*. At that time He was not less than 100 years old. He had great-grandchildren, but He looked just like a boy. Kṛṣṇa, God, never becomes old. That is His Supreme power. And if you want to search out Kṛṣṇa by studying the Vedic literature, then you will be baffled. It may be possible, but it is very difficult. But you can very easily learn about Him from His devotee. His devotee can deliver Him to you: "Here He is, take Him." That is the potency of Kṛṣṇa's devotees.

Originally there was only one *Veda*, and there was no necessity of reading it. People were so intelligent and had such sharp memories that by once hearing from the lips of the spiritual master they would understand. They would immediately grasp the whole purport. But 5,000 years ago Vyāsadeva put the *Vedas* in writing for the people in this age, *Kali-yuga*. He knew that eventually the people would be short-lived, their memories would be very poor and their intelligence would not be very sharp. "Therefore, let me teach this Vedic knowledge in writing." He divided the *Vedas* into four: *Ṛk, Sāma, Atharva,* and *Yajus*. Then he gave the charge of these *Vedas* to his different disciples. He then thought of the less intelligent class of men, *strī, śūdra* and *dvija-bandhu*. He considered the woman class and *śūdra* class (worker class) and *dvija-bandhu*. *Dvija-bandhu* refers to those who are born in a high family but who are not properly qualified. A man born in the family of a *brāhmaṇa*, who is not qualified as a *brāhmaṇa*, is called *dvija-bandhu*. For these persons, he compiled *Mahābhārata*, called the history of India, and the eighteen *Purānas*. These are all Vedic literatures: the *Purāṇas*, the *Mahābhārata*, the four *Vedas*, and the *Upaniṣads*. The *Upaniṣads* are part of the *Vedas*. Then Vyāsadeva summarized all Vedic knowledge for scholars and philosophers in what is called the *Vedānta-sūtra*. This is the last word of the *Vedas*. Vyāsadeva personally wrote *Vedānta-sūtra* under the instructions of Nārada, his *Guru Mahārāj*, spiritual master, but still he was not satisfied. That is a long story, described in the *Śrīmad-Bhāgavatam*. Vedavyāsa was not very satisfied even after compiling many *Purāṇas, Upaniṣads*, and even after *Vedānta-sūtra*. Then his spiritual master, Nārada, instructed him, "You explain *Vedānta*." *Vedānta* means Ultimate Knowledge, and the Ultimate Knowledge is Kṛṣṇa. Kṛṣṇa says that throughout all the *Vedas* one has to understand Kṛṣṇa. *Vedānta-kṛd veda-vid eva cāham*. Kṛṣṇa says, "I am the Compiler of *Vedānta*, and I am the Knower of the *Vedas*." Therefore the Ultimate Objective is Kṛṣṇa. That is explained in all the Vaiṣṇava commentaries on *Vedānta* philosophy. We Gauḍīya Vaiṣṇavas have our commentary on *Vedānta* philosophy, called *Govinda-bhaṣya* by Baladeva Vidyābhūṣaṇa. Similarly, Rāmānujācārya has a commentary and Madhvācārya has one. The version of Śaṅkarācārya is not the only commentary. There are many *Vedānta* commentaries, but because the Vaiṣṇavas did not present the first *Vedānta* commentary, people are under the wrong impression that Śaṅkarācārya's is the only *Vedānta* commentary. Besides that, Vyāsadeva himself wrote the perfect *Vedānta* commentary, *Śrīmad-Bhāgavatam*. *Śrīmad-Bhāgavatam* also begins with the first words of the Vedānta-sūtra*: janmādyasya yataḥ*. And that *janmādyasya yataḥ* is fully explained in the *Śrīmad-Bhāgavatam*. The *Vedānta-sūtra* simply hints at what is *Brahman*, the Absolute Truth: "The Absolute Truth is that from Whom everything emanates." This is a summary, but it is explained in detail in *Śrīmad-Bhāgavatam*. If everything is emanating from the Absolute Truth, then what is the nature of the Absolute Truth? That is explained in *Śrīmad-Bhāgavatam*. The Absolute Truth must be conscious. *Svarāṭ*. He is Self-effulgent. We develop our consciousness and knowledge by receiving knowledge from others, but for Him it is said that He is Self-effulgent. The whole summary of Vedic knowledge is the *Vedānta-sūtra*, and the *Vedānta-sūtra* is explained by the writer himself in the *Śrīmad-Bhāgavatam*. We finally request those who are actually after Vedic knowledge to try to understand the explanation of all Vedic knowledge from the *Śrīmad-Bhāgavatam* and the *Bhagavad-gītā*.

Invocation

ॐ पूर्णमदः पूर्णमिदं पूर्णात् पूर्णमुदच्यते ।
पूर्णस्य पूर्णमादाय पूर्णमेवावशिष्यते ॥

om pūrṇam adaḥ pūrṇam idaṁ
pūrṇāt pūrṇam udacyate
pūrṇasya pūrṇam ādāya
pūrṇam evāvaśiṣyate.

om—the Complete Whole; *pūrṇam*—perfectly complete; *adaḥ*—that; *pūrṇam*—perfectly complete; *idam*—this phenomenal world; *pūrṇāt*—from the all perfect; *pūrṇam*—complete unit; *udacyate*—produced; *pūrṇasya*—of the Complete Whole; *pūrṇam*—completely all; *ādāya*—having been taken away; *pūrṇam*—the complete balance; *eva*—even; *avaśiṣyate*—is remaining.

TRANSLATION

The Personality of Godhead is perfect and complete. And because He is completely perfect, all emanations from Him, such as this phenomenal world, are perfectly equipped as a complete whole. Whatever is produced of the complete whole is also complete by itself. And because He is the Complete Whole, even though so many complete units emanate from Him, He remains the complete balance.

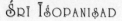

PURPORT

The Complete Whole, or the Supreme Absolute Truth, is the complete Personality of Godhead. Impersonal *Brahman* forms an incomplete realization of the Absolute Complete, and so also does the conception of *Paramātman*, the Supersoul. The Supreme Personality of Godhead is *sac-cid-ānanda-vigraha*: impersonal *Brahman* realization is the realization of His *sat*, or eternity aspect, and *Paramātman*, Supersoul realization, is the realization of His *sat* and *cit*, eternity and knowledge aspects. But realization of the Personality of Godhead is realization of all the transcendental features, *sat*, *cit*, and *ānanda*, or bliss. In the Personal concept, this is realized in complete form (*vigraha*). And so the Complete Whole is not formless. If He is formless, or if He is less than His creation in any other thing, He cannot be complete. The Complete Whole must have everything, both within our experience and beyond our experience. Otherwise He cannot be complete.

The Complete Whole Personality of Godhead has immense potencies, and all of them are as complete as He is. Therefore this phenomenal or material world is also complete by itself. The twenty-four elements of which this material universe is a temporary manifestation are completely adjusted to produce complete things necessary for the maintenance and subsistence of this universe. No extraneous effort by any other unit is required for this maintenance. The universe has its own time, fixed by the energy of the Complete Whole, and when that time is complete this temporary manifestation will be annihilated by the complete arrangement of the Complete.

There is complete facility for the small complete units, namely the living beings, to realize the Complete; and all forms of incompleteness are experienced only on account of incomplete knowledge of the Complete. The human form of life is a complete manifestation of the consciousness of the living being, which is obtained after evolving through 8,400,000 species of life in the cycle of birth and death. If a human being does not realize his completeness within the Complete in this life of full consciousness, he loses the chance of realizing his completeness, and is put again into the cycle of evolution by the law of material Nature.

Because we do not know that there is a complete arrangement in Nature for our maintenance, we make efforts to utilize the resources of Nature to create a so-called complete life of sense enjoyment. This misleading life of sense-enjoyment is called illusion, because the living entity cannot enjoy the life of the senses without being dovetailed with the Complete Whole. For example, the hand of a body is a complete unit as long as it is attached to the complete body. When the hand is detached from the body, it may appear like a hand, but actually it has none of the potency of a hand. Similarly, the living beings are parts and parcels of the Complete Whole; and as long as the parts and parcels are detached from the Complete Whole, the illusory representation of completeness is not enough to bring the desired result.

The completeness of human life can only be realized when the human form of life is engaged in the service of the Complete Whole. Any service in this world, whether social, political, communal, international, or even inter-planetary, will remain incomplete unless and until it is dovetailed with the Complete Whole. And, when everything is dovetailed with the Complete Whole, the attached parts and parcels also become complete in themselves.

Mantra One

ईशा वास्यमिदꣳ सर्वं यत्किञ्च जगत्यां जगत् ।
तेन त्यक्तेन भुञ्जीथा मा गृधः कस्य स्विद् धनम् ॥ १ ॥

īśāvāsyam idaṁ sarvaṁ
yat kiñca jagatyāṁ jagat
tena tyaktena bhuñjīthā
mā gṛdhaḥ kasya svid dhanam.

īśā—by the Lord; *vāsyam*—controlled; *idam*—this; *sarvam*—all; *yat*—whatever; *kim*—it (is); *ca*—and; *jagatyām*—within the universe; *jagat*—all that is animate or inanimate; *tena*—by Him; *tyaktena*—set apart quota; *bhuñjīthāḥ*—must you accept; *mā*—do not; *gṛdhaḥ*—make into use; *kasya svid*—whom does it belong; *dhanam*—things necessary.

TRANSLATION

Everything animate or inanimate that is within the universe is controlled and owned by the Lord. One should therefore accept only those things necessary for himself, which are set aside as his quota, and one must not accept other things, knowing well to Whom they belong.

PURPORT

The Vedic knowledge is infallible because it comes down through the perfect disciplic succession of spiritual masters beginning with the Lord Himself. The Vedic knowledge is received from the transcendental sources, and the first word was spoken by the Lord Himself. The words spoken by the Lord are called *apauruṣeya*, not delivered by any person of the mundane world. A living being of the mundane world has four defects, which are: 1. that he must commit mistakes, 2. he must sometimes be illusioned, 3. he must try to cheat others, and 4. he is endowed with imperfect senses. With these four principles of imperfection one cannot deliver perfect information in the matter of all-pervading knowledge. The *Vedas* are not known like that. The Vedic knowledge was originally imparted into the heart of Brahmā the first created living being, and Brahmā in his turn disseminated the knowledge to his sons and disciples, who have continued the process down through history.

The Lord being *pūrṇam,* or all-perfect, there is no chance of His being subjected to the laws of material Nature, while the living entities and inanimate objects are all controlled by the laws of Nature, and thus, ultimately, by the potency of the Lord. This *Īśopaniṣad* is a part of the *Yajur Veda,* and as such it contains information as to the proprietorship of all things that exist within the universe.

This point is confirmed by the *Bhagavad-gītā,* in the Seventh Chapter, where *parā* and *aparā prakṛti* are discussed: The elements of Nature—earth, fire, water, air, sky, mind, intelligence and ego—all belong to the inferior or material energy of the Lord, whereas the living being, the organic energy, is the superior energy, the *parā prakṛti,* of the Lord. Both the *prakṛtis* or energies are emanations from the Lord, and ultimately He is the Controller of everything that exists. There is nothing in the universe which does not belong either to the *parā* or the *aparā prakṛti,* and therefore everything is under the proprietary right of the Supreme Being.

The Supreme Being, the Absolute Personality of Godhead, being the complete Person, has the complete and perfect intelligence to adjust everything by His different potencies. The

Supreme Being is often compared with fire, and everything—organic and inorganic—is compared with the heat and light of the fire. The fire distributes energy in the form of heat and light, and likewise the Lord displays His energy in different ways. And He remains the ultimate Controller, Sustainer and Dictator over everything. He is full of all potencies, the Knower of everything, the Benefactor of everyone, and is full of all inconceivable opulences: power, wealth, fame, beauty, knowledge and renunciation.

One should therefore be intelligent enough to know that except for the Lord no one is the proprietor of anything; one should accept only the things which are set aside by the Lord as his quota. The cow, for example, gives milk, but she does not drink the milk. Her milk is designated as food for the human being. The cow eats grass and straw but does not drink her own milk. Such is the arrangement of the Lord, and we should be satisfied with the things that have been very kindly set aside for us by Him. We should always consider to Whom the things that we possess actually belong.

Take, for example, our dwelling house, which is made of earth, wood, stone, iron, cement, and so many other material things. If we think in terms of *Śrī Īśopaniṣad,* then we must know that we cannot produce any of the above-mentioned building materials ourselves. We can simply bring them together and transform them into different shapes by our labor. A laborer cannot claim to be the proprietor of a thing just because he has worked hard to manufacture it.

There is always this great quarrel between the laborers and the capitalists in present-day society. The quarrel has now taken an international shape, and the world is in danger. Men face each other in enmity just like cats and dogs snarling.

Śrī Īśopaniṣad cannot give advice to the cats and dogs, but It delivers the message of Godhead to man through the bona fide *ācāryas,* or holy teachers. And the human race may take this Vedic wisdom from *Śrī Īśopaniṣad:* that no one should quarrel over material possessions. One must be satisfied by whatever privileges are given to him by the mercy of the Lord. There can be no peace if the communist or the capitalist or any other party claims to be the proprietor of the resources of Nature, which are entirely the property of the Lord.

The capitalist cannot curb down the communist simply by political maneuvering, nor can the communist defeat the capitalist simply by fighting for the stolen bread. If they do not recognize the proprietorship of the Supreme Personality of Godhead, then all the property which they claim to be their own is stolen, and therefore they shall be liable to punishment by the laws of Nature. The Bomb is in the hands of both the communists and the capitalists, and if both do not recognize the proprietorship of the Supreme Lord, it is sure and certain that, ultimately, the Bomb will ruin both parties. Therefore, in order to save themselves, both must follow the instruction of *Śrī Īśopaniṣad,* and thus bring peace to the world.

Human beings are not meant for quarreling like cats and dogs. They must be intelligent enough to realize the importance of human life, and to realize the aim of human life. The Vedic literature is meant for humanity and not for cats and dogs. Cats and dogs can kill other animals for food and for that there is no question of sin on their part. But if a man kills an animal for the satisfaction of his uncontrolled taste buds, he is responsible for breaking the laws of Nature, and therefore he must be punished.

There is a standard of life for human beings which cannot

apply to the animals. The tiger does not eat rice, wheat or cow's milk because it has been given its quota of foodstuff in the shape of animal food. There are many animals and birds who are either vegetarian or non-vegetarian, but none of them transgress the laws of Nature as they have been ordained by the will of the Lord. Amongst the living beings—whether animals or birds or reptiles—there is strict adherence to the laws of Nature, and therefore there is no question of sin for them, nor are the Vedic instructions meant for them. Human life alone, then, is a life of responsibility.

It is also wrong to consider that simply by becoming a vegetarian one can save himself from transgressing the laws of Nature. Vegetables also have life. One life is meant to feed another living being, and that is the law of Nature. One should not be proud of being a strict vegetarian. The point is to recognize the Supreme Lord. The animals have no developed consciousness to recognize the Lord, but a human being is sufficiently intelligent to take lessons from the Vedic literature, and thereby know how the laws of Nature are working, and derive profit out of such knowledge. If a man neglects the instruction of the Vedic literature, his life is very risky. The human being is therefore required to recognize the authority of the Supreme Lord. He must be a devotee of the Lord. He must offer everything to the service of the Lord and partake of only the remnants of foodstuff offered to the Lord. That will make him able to discharge his duty properly. In the *Bhagavad-gītā* the Lord directly states that He accepts the vegetable foodstuffs from the hands of a pure devotee. Therefore a human being should not only become a strict vegetarian, but he should also be a devotee of the Lord, and offer to the Lord all his food, and only then partake of the *prasādam,* or mercy of God.

Such a devotee can properly discharge the duty of human life. Those who do not do so are eating only sins, and thus will be subjected to the different types of distress which are the result of the various sins.

The root of sin is deliberate disobedience to the laws of Nature, through not recognizing the proprietorship of the Lord. Disobedience to the laws of Nature or disobedience to the order of the Lord will bring ruin to the human being. On the other hand, if one is sober and knows the laws of Nature, without being influenced by unnecessary attachment or abhorrence, he is sure to be recognized again by the Lord, and thus become eligible for going back to Godhead, back to the eternal Home.

Mantra Two

कुर्वन्नेवेह कर्माणि जिजीविषेच्छतꣳ समाः ।
एवं त्वयि नान्यथेतोऽस्ति न कर्म लिप्यते नरे ॥ २ ॥

kurvann eveha karmāṇi
jijīviṣec chataṁ samāḥ
evaṁ tvayi nānyatheto'sti
na karma lipyate nare.

kurvan—doing continuously; *eva*—thus; *iha*—during this span of life; *karmāṇi*—work; *jijīviṣet*—one should desire to live; *śatam*—one hundred; *samāḥ*—years; *evam*—so living; *tvayi*—unto you; *na*—no; *anyathā*—alternative; *itaḥ*—from this path; *asti*—there is; *na*—not; *karma*—work; *lipyate*—can be bound; *nare*—unto a man.

TRANSLATION

One may aspire to live for hundreds of years if he continuously goes on doing work in that way, because that sort of work will not bind him to the law of karma. And there is no alternative to this way for man.

PURPORT

No one wants to die, and everyone wants to live for as long as he can drag on. This temperament is not only visible individually, but also it is visible collectively in the community, society and nation. There is a hard struggle for life in every class of living entities, and the *Veda* says that this is quite natural for the living being. The living being is eternal by nature, but due to his bondage in the material existence he has to change his body from one to another. This process is called transmigration of the soul. This transmigration is also called *Karma-bandhana*, or being bound by one's own work. The living entity has to work for his livelihood because that is the law of material Nature, and if he does not act according to the prescribed duties of his particular life he transgresses the law of Nature, making himself bound more and more in the cycle of birth and death.

The cycle of birth and death is present in life other than the human form. When the living entity gets the chance for human life, however, it is his chance to get free from the chain of the law of *karma*. *Karma*, *akarma*, and *vikarma* are principles very clearly described in the *Bhagavad-gītā*. Actions which are done in terms of the prescribed duties mentioned in the revealed Scriptures are called *karma*. Actions which make one free from the cycle of birth and death are called *akarma*. And actions which are performed by the misuse of one's freedom, thereby directing oneself toward the lower regions of life, are called *vikarma.*

Of these three categories of activities, the one which makes one free from the cycle of further bondage to *karma* is preferred by intelligent men. Ordinary men want to perform good work in order to be recognized and to achieve some status of life in this world or in heaven, but more advanced men want to be free altogether from the actions and reactions of work. Intelligent men know well that both good and bad works are equally causes of the material miseries of life. They therefore seek to do work which will free them from the reactions of good and bad work. This freedom from good and bad work is ascertained herewith in *Śrī Īśopaniṣad.*

The instruction of *Śrī Īśopaniṣad* is better explained in the *Bhagavad-gītā,* sometimes called the *Gītopaniṣad,* the cream of all the *Upaniṣads.* In the *Bhagavad-gītā,* the Personality of Godhead says that no one can attain the state of *naiṣkarma* or *akarma* without beginning the prescribed duties mentioned in the Vedic literature. The Vedic literature can regulate the working energy of the human being in such a way that one can gradually realize the authority of the Supreme Being. When one realizes the authority of the Personality of Godhead, it is to be understood that he has attained the stage of positive knowledge. At this purified stage of life, where the modes of Nature— namely goodness, passion and ignorance—cannot act, one is enabled to work on the basis of *naiṣkarma,* or work which does not bind one to the cycle of birth and death.

Factually, no one has to do anything more than to render devotional service to the Lord. In the lower stage of life, however, one can not at once adopt the activities of devotional service, nor can one completely stop reactionary work. A conditioned soul is accustomed to working for sense gratification, for his own selfish interest, immediate or extended. An ordinary man wants to work for his own sense enjoyment, and when the principle of sense enjoyment is extended from the individual to include the collective society, nation, or humanity in general, it assumes various attractive names such as altruism, socialism, communism, nationalism, humanitarianism, etc. These isms are certainly very attractive forms of *Karma-bandhana,* the bondage of one's own work, but the Vedic instruction of *Śrī Īśopaniṣad* is as follows: if you actually live for any of the above isms, make them God-centered. There is no harm in becoming a family man, an altruist, socialist, communist, nationalist, or humanitarian—provided all such activities are executed in relation with *īśāvāsya,* the God-centered conception.

God-centered activities are evaluated in the *Bhagavad-gītā* as being so rich that even a little bit of them can save one from the greatest danger. The greatest danger of life is to glide down again into the evolutionary cycle of birth and death. If some way or other a man misses the spiritual opportunity offered by his human form of life, and thus glides down again into the evolutionary cycle, it must be considered the most regrettable incidence, although foolish man cannot see this, due to his defective senses. *Śrī Īśopaniṣad* advises us, therefore, to exert our energy in the *īśāvāsya* spirit, and in that engagement we may wish to live for many, many years. Otherwise, one's long life is no better than that of a tree, which is also a living being, and which lives for hundreds and hundreds of years. There is no point in living a long time like the trees, or breathing like the bellows, or begetting children like the hog and the dog, or eating like the camel. Even a humble life, with God-centered activities, is more valuable than the colossal hoax of so-called altruism or socialism without any relation to God.

When activities such as altruism are executed in the spirit of *Śrī Īśopaniṣad,* every one of them becomes a form of *karma-yoga,* as is recommended in the *Bhagavad-gītā.* And that guarantees the executor against the dangers of the evolutionary process of birth and death. Such God-centered activities, even though half-finished, are still good for the executor, because they will guarantee him the human form of life in his next birth. In this way he can have another chance to improve his position on the path of liberation.

Mantra Three

असुर्या नाम ते लोका अन्धेन तमसाऽऽवृताः ।
ताँस्ते प्रेत्याभिगच्छन्ति ये के चात्महनो जनाः ॥ ३ ॥

asuryā nāma te lokā
andhena tamasāvṛtāḥ
tāṁs te pretyābhigacchanti
ye ke cātma-hano janāḥ.

asuryāḥ—meant for the *asuras; nāma*—famous by the name; *te*—those; *lokāḥ*—planets; *andhena*—ignorance; *tamasā*—darkness; *āvṛtāḥ*—covered by; *tān*—there; *te*—they; *pretya*—after death; *abhigacchanti*—do enter into; *ye*—anyone; *ke*—everyone; *ca*—and; *ātma-hanaḥ*—the killer of the soul; *janāḥ*—persons.

TRANSLATION

The killer of the soul, whoever he may be, must enter into the planets known as the worlds of the faithless, full of darkness and ignorance.

PURPORT

A human life is distinguished from animal life on account of its heavy responsibilities. Those who are cognizant of these responsibilities and work in that spirit are called *suras,* the godly. And those who are either neglectful of the responsibilities or who have no information about them are called the *asuras,* or demons. There are only these two kinds of human beings all over the universe. In the *Ṛg Veda* it is stated that the *suras* always aim at the Lotus Feet of the Supreme Lord Viṣṇu, and act accordingly. Their ways are as illuminated as the path of the Sun.

Intelligent human beings must always remember that this particular form of body is obtained after an evolution of many millions of years of transmigration of the soul. This material world is sometimes compared with an ocean, and this human body is compared with a solid boat, designed to cross over the ocean. The Vedic Scriptures and the *ācāryas,* or saintly teachers, are compared with the expert boatman, and the facilities of a human body are compared with favorable breezes, which can help the boat smoothly ply to the desired destination. If, with all these facilities, a person does not fully utilize his human life for self realization, such an *asura* must be considered *ātma-hana,* a killer of the soul. The killer of the soul is destined to enter into the darkest region of ignorance to suffer perpetually, and here is a warning by *Śrī Īśopaniṣad* in clear terms.

There are swine, dogs, camels, asses, etc. whose economic necessities are just as important as ours. But the economic problems of these animals are solved under nasty conditions, while the human being is given all facilities for comfortable life by the laws of Nature, because the human form of life is more important than animal life. And why is man given a better life than the swine and other animals? Why is a highly placed servant given all the facilities of comfortable life, rather than an ordinary clerk? The answer is that the highly placed officer has to discharge duties of a higher nature. Similarly, the human being has higher duties in life than the animals who are engaged always in the business of feeding their hungry stomachs.

The modern soul-killing civilization has only increased the problems of a hungry stomach. We approach some polished animal, a modern civilized man, and he says that he wants to work for the satisfaction of the stomach and there is no necessity for self realization. But the laws of Nature are so cruel that in spite of his eagerness to work hard for his stomach, there is always the question of unemployment, even after denouncing the prospect of self-realization.

We are given this human form of life not to work hard like the ass, the swine and the dog, but to attain the highest perfection of life. If we do not care for self-realization, it is by the law of Nature that we have to work very hard even though we do not want to do so. In this age the human being has been forced to work hard like the ass and the bull, pulling carts. These are some of the examples of the regions where an *asura* is sent to work, revealed by this verse of *Śrī Īśopaniṣad.* If a man fails to discharge his duties as a human being, he is forced to transmigrate to the planets called *asurya* in the degraded species of life, to work hard in ignorance and darkness.

In the *Bhagavad-gītā* it is also stated that the half-self-realized men who in their previous lives could not complete the process of approaching Godhead but had sincerely tried for it—in other words, those who failed to attain success in realizing their relation with God—are given the chance of appearing in the family of *śuci* or *śrīmata. Śuci* means a spiritually advanced *Brāhmaṇa,* and *śrīmata* means a *Vaiśya,* or member of the mercantile community. This means that such fallen candidates are given a better chance for culturing self-realization on account of their sincere efforts in past lives. If the fallen candidates are given the chance of taking birth in respectable noble families, we can hardly imagine the state of those who have completely achieved success in the attempt.

Simply to make an attempt for realizing God is to guarantee that the next birth will be in a noble family. But those who do not make any such attempt at all, and who want to be covered by illusion, too materialistic and attached to material enjoyment, must enter into the darkest region of hell, as is confirmed in all the Vedic literature.

Such materialistic *asuras* sometimes make a show of religiousness with the ultimate aim of material prosperity. The *Bhagavad-gītā,* however, rebukes them as men called great on the strength of false perfection, empowered by the votes of the ignorant and by material wealth. Such *asuras,* devoid of self realization and the conception of *īśāvāsya,* the Lord, are sure to enter into the darkest regions.

The conclusion is that we are not meant only for solving economic problems on a tottering platform, but we are also meant for solving the problems of the material life into which we have been placed by the conditions of Nature.

Mantra Four

अनेजदेकं मनसो जवीयो नैनद्देवा आप्नुवन् पूर्वमर्षत् ।
तद्धावतोऽन्यानत्येति तिष्ठत्तस्मिन्नपो मातरिश्वा दधाति ॥ ४ ॥

anejad ekaṁ manaso javīyo
nainad devā āpnuvan pūrvam arṣat
tad dhāvato 'nyān atyeti tiṣṭhat
tasminn apo mātariśvā dadhāti.

anejat—fixed up; *ekam*—one; *manasaḥ*—more than the mind; *javīyaḥ*—speedy; no—not; *enat*—this Supreme Lord; *devāḥ*—the demigods like Indra, etc.; *āpnuvan*—can approach; *pūrvam*—the first of all; *arṣat*—one who knows everything; *tat*—that; *dhāvataḥ*—those who are running; *anyān*—others; *atyeti*—surpasses; *tiṣṭhat*—although placed; *tasmin*—in one place; *apaḥ*—water; *mātariśvā*—the gods who control air and rains; *dadhāti*—execute.

TRANSLATION

The Personality of Godhead, although fixed in His Abode, is more swift than the mind, and can overcome all others running. The powerful demigods cannot approach Him. Although in one place, He has control over those who supply the air and rain. He surpasses all in excellence.

PURPORT

The Supreme Lord, Who is the Absolute Personality of Godhead, is not knowable even to the greatest philosopher through mental speculation. He can be known only by His devotees through His mercy. In the *Brahma-saṁhitā* it is said that the non-devotee philosopher who can travel at the speed of the mind, or at the velocity of the air, and who can travel in space for hundreds of years, will find the Absolute still far, far away from him. As described in the *Upaniṣads,* the Absolute Personality of Godhead has His transcendental Abode, known as *Kṛṣṇa-loka,* where He remains, engaged in His Pastimes. But by His inconceivable potency He can simultaneously reach every part of the creative energy. In the *Viṣṇu Purāṇa* this potency is compared with the light and heat of the fire. The fire can distribute its light and heat from one place, and similarly the Absolute Personality of Godhead, although fixed up in His transcendental Abode, can diffuse His different energies everywhere.

Such energies are innumerable, but principally they are classified into three: the internal potency, the marginal potency, and the external potency. In each and every one of them, there are hundreds and millions of sub-headings. The dominating demigods who are empowered to have control over the administration of natural phenomena such as the air, light, rain, etc. are all classified within the marginal potency of the Absolute Person. The living beings, including humans, are also products of the marginal potency of the Lord. The material world is the creation of the external potency of the Lord, and the spiritual sky, where the Kingdom of God is situated, is the manifestation of His internal potency.

The different energies of the Supreme Lord are represented everywhere by His different potencies. Although there is no difference between Him and His energies, still one should not wrongly conclude that the Supreme Lord, being thus distributed everywhere, has His Personal existence solely in the impersonal *Brahman.* Men are accustomed to reach conclusions only according to their own capacity to understand. But the Supreme Lord is not subject to our limited capacity to understand Him. It is for this reason that the *Upaniṣads* warn us: no one can approach the Lord by his own limited potency.

In the *Bhagavad-gītā,* the Lord says that no one, not even the great *ṛṣis* and *suras,* can know Him. So what is there to say of the *asuras,* who are not even qualified to understand the ways of the Lord? All these words mentioned in Mantra Four of *Śrī Īśopaniṣad* suggest very clearly that the Absolute Truth is ultimately the Absolute Person; otherwise there would have been no necessity of mentioning so many varied things in support of His Personal features.

Individual parts and parcels of the potencies of the Lord, although having all the symptoms of the Lord Himself, have limited spheres of activities, and therefore are all limited. The parts and parcels are never equal to the whole. Therefore the parts and parcels cannot appreciate the full potency of the Lord. Foolish and ignorant living beings who are parts and parcels of the Lord, under the influence of the material energy, try to make a conjecture on the transcendental position of the Lord. *Śrī Īśopaniṣad* warns them not to make any mental speculation about the identity of the Lord. Try to know the Transcendence from the superior source of the *Vedas,* which is already in knowledge of the Transcendence.

Every part of the Complete Whole is endowed with some particular energy to act, and forgetfulness by that part of his particular activities is called *māyā,* illusion. *Śrī Īśopaniṣad* has therefore, from the very beginning, warned us that we should be careful to play the part designated for us by the Lord. This, however, does not mean that the individual soul has no initiative of his own. Because he is the part and parcel of the Lord he must have the initiative of the Lord as well. Proper use of one's initiative, active nature, with intelligence to understand that everything is but the potency of the Lord, can lead one to the revival of his original consciousness, which was lost on account of association with *māyā,* the external energy.

All power is obtained from the Lord, and therefore each particular power must be utilized to execute the will of the Lord, and not otherwise. The Lord can be known by one who has adopted a submissive attitude. Perfect knowledge means to know the Lord in all His features, to know about His potencies and how such potencies are working by His will. These things are exclusively described by the Lord in the *Bhagavad-gītā,* which is the essence of all the *Upaniṣads.*

Mantra Five

तदेजति तन्नैजति तद्द् दूरे तद्वन्तिके ।
तदन्तरस्य सर्वस्य तदु सर्वस्यास्य बाह्यतः ॥ ५ ॥

tad ejati tan naijati
tad dūre tad vantike
tad antarasya sarvasya
tad u sarvasyāsya bāhyataḥ.

tat—this Supreme Lord; *ejati*—does walk; *tat*—He; *na*—not; *ejati*—does walk; *tat*—He (is); *dūre*—far away; *tat*—He (is); *u*—also; *antike*—very near; *tat*—He (is); *antar*—within; *asya*—of this; *sarvasya*—all; *tat*—He (is); *u*—also; *sarvasya*—all; *asya*—of this; *bāhyataḥ*—external to.

TRANSLATION

The Supreme Lord walks and does not walk. He is far away, but He is very near as well. He is within everything, and again He is outside of everything.

PURPORT

Here is an explanation of the Supreme Lord's transcendental activities by His inconceivable potencies. There are two sets of contradictory words mentioned herein to prove the inconceivable potency of the Lord. He walks, and He does not walk. These two phrases are contradictory. If someone can walk then it is improper to say that he cannot walk. These contradictions show the inconceivable power of God. With our limited fund of knowledge we cannot accommodate such things, and therefore the Lord is conceived in terms of our limited powers of understanding. The impersonalist philosophers of the *māyā-vāda* school accept only the impersonalist part of the Lord's activities, and refute His Personal feature. The *Bhāgavata* school, however, accepts the Lord in both ways, i.e., as Personal and impersonal. And the *Bhāgavatas* also accept His inconceivable potencies. Without inconceivable potency there is no meaning to the words *Supreme Lord.*

We should not take it for granted that because we cannot see God before our eyes there is therefore no personal existence of the Lord. To refute this sort of argument, *Śrī Īśopaniṣad* warns us that the Lord is far away from us, but He is very near to us also. The Abode of the Lord is beyond the material sky. We have no means to measure even the material sky. If just the material sky is so far, far away from us, then what of the spiritual sky, which is beyond the material sky altogether? That the spiritual sky is situated far, far away from the material world is further confirmed in the *Bhagavad-gītā.* But, in spite of the Lord's being so far away, He can at once, within less than a second, descend before us with a speed more powerful than the mind or the air. He can walk so quickly that no one can surpass Him. This fact has already been described in the previous verse.

When the Personality of Godhead thus comes before us, however, we neglect Him. This negligence on the part of the foolish people is condemned by the Lord in the *Bhagavad-gītā*. The Lord says that the foolish deride Him, taking Him to be one of the mortal beings. But He is not a mortal being, nor does He come before us with a body produced of material Nature. There are many so-called scholars who say that when the Lord descends, He does so in a body of matter, just like an ordinary living being. Such foolish men place the Lord on a level equal to that of the ordinary man, not knowing His inconceivable power.

Because He is full of inconceivable potencies, God can accept our service through any sort of medium, and He can convert His different potencies according to His own will. The unbelievers argue that the Lord cannot incarnate Himself, or if at all, He descends in a form of material energy. This argument is nullified if we accept His inconceivable potencies as realities. Even if He appears before us in the form of material energy, it is quite possible for Him to convert the material energy into spiritual energy. The source of the energies being one and the same, the energies can be utilized suitably according to the will of that energetic Source. For example, the Lord appears in the Form of *Ārca*, or Deities supposedly made of earth or stone. These forms, engraved from wood or stone or any other matter, are not idols, however, as is held by the iconoclasts.

In the present state of our imperfect material existence we cannot see the Supreme Lord on account of our imperfect vision. But still, those devotees who want to see Him by means of material vision are favored by the Lord, Who appears in so-called material form to accept the devotees' service. This does not mean that such devotees, who are in the lowest stage of devotional service, are worshiping an idol. In fact, they are worshiping the Lord, Who has agreed to appear before them in a particular way which is approachable by them. This *Arca* Form is not fashioned in terms of the order or whim of the worshiper. It is eternally existent with all Its paraphernalia. This can be actually felt by a sincere devotee, but not by an atheist.

In the *Bhagavad-gītā* the Lord says that He treats His devotee in proportion to the degree of surrender made by the devotee. He reserves the right not to expose Himself to anyone and everyone, except those who surrender unto Him. Therefore, for the surrendered soul, He is always within reach, whereas for the non-surrendered soul, He is far, far away, and cannot be approached.

There are two words in the revealed Scriptures which are important in this connection: *saguṇa* and *nirguṇa*—with qualities and without qualities. *Saguṇa* does not mean that the Lord becomes subject to the laws of material Nature when He appears, although He has qualities and appears in the material form. For Him there is no difference between material and spiritual energies, because He is the Source of such energies. He is the Controller of the different energies, and as such He cannot at any time be under their influence, as we are. The material energy works according to His direction, and therefore He can use the material energy for His purpose, but without ever being influenced by any of the qualities of His energies. Nor for this purpose does He become a formless entity at any time. Ultimately He is the eternal Form, the Primeval Lord.

And the impersonal representation, or *Brahman* effulgence, is the glow of His Personal rays, as the Sun's rays are the glow of the Sun god.

When the boy saint Prahlāda Mahārāj was in the presence of his atheist father, his father asked him, "Where is your God?" The child Prahlāda replied that God resides everywhere. The father then angrily asked whether his God was within the pillar of the palace, and the child said yes. At once the atheist king broke the pillar in front of him into pieces, at which the Lord appeared as Nṛsiṁha (the half-man, half-lion Incarnation) from within the pillar, and killed the atheist king. This means that the Lord is within everything, which is created by His different energies. And by His inconceivable power He can appear at any place in order to favor His sincere devotee. Lord Nṛsiṁha appeared from within the pillar not at the order of the atheist king, but by the wish of the devotee Prahlāda. An atheist cannot order the Lord to appear, but to show mercy to His devotee the Lord can appear anywhere and everywhere.

The *Bhagavad-gītā* confirms this, in the statement that the Lord appears to vanquish the unbelievers and to protect the believers. To vanquish an unbeliever, of course, the Lord has sufficient energies and agents who can do the work, but to favor the devotee is a pleasing task for Him, and therefore He descends as an incarnation. He does so only to favor His devotees, then, and not for any other purpose.

In the *Brahma-saṁhitā* it is said that Govinda, the Primeval Lord, enters everything by His plenary portion. He enters the universe as well as the atom of the universe. He is outside in the *Virāṭa* Form, and He is within as *Antaryāmi*. As *Antaryāmi* He is witness of everything that we are doing, and He gives us the result of our actions as *karma-phala*. We ourselves may forget what we have done in previous lives, but because the

Lord is the witness of our actions, the result of our actions is always there, and we have to undergo the reactions all the same.

In fact there is nothing except God within and without. Everything is manifested of His different energies, like the heat and light of fire, which means there is a oneness among the diverse energies. In spite of this oneness, however, the Lord enjoys in His Personal Form all that is enjoyable to the little senses of the little part and parcel living entities.

Mantra Six

यस्तु सर्वाणि भूतान्यात्मन्येवानुपश्यति ।
सर्वभूतेषु चात्मानं ततो न विजुगुप्सते ॥ ६ ॥

yas tu sarvāṇi bhūtāny
ātmany evānupaśyati
sarva-bhūteṣu cātmānaṁ
tato na vijugupsate.

yaḥ—a person; *tu*—but; *sarvāṇi*—all; *bhūtāni*—living entities; *ātmani*—in relation with the Supreme Lord; *eva*—only; *anupaśyati*—observes in a systematic way; *sarva-bhūteṣu*—in every living being; *ca*—and; *ātmānam*—the Supersoul; *tataḥ*—thereafter; *na*—not; *vijugupsate*—hates anyone.

TRANSLATION

A person who sees everything in relation to the Supreme Lord, and sees all entities as His parts

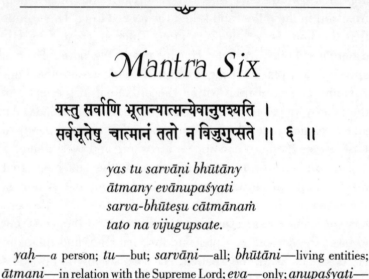

and parcels, and who sees the Supreme Lord within everything, never hates anything, nor any being.

PURPORT

Here is an explanation of the *Mahābhāgavata*, the great personality who sees everything in relation to the Supreme Personality of Godhead. There are three stages of realizing the presence of the Supreme Lord: The *kaniṣṭha adhikāri*, the person who is in the lowest stage of realization of the Lord, goes to one place of worship, such as a temple, church, or mosque, in terms of his particular type of religious faith, and worships there in terms of the scriptural injunctions. Such devotees think that the Lord is there at the place of worship and nowhere else. Such devotees cannot recognize who is in what position in the devotional line, or in terms of realization of the Supreme Lord. They follow the routine formulas and sometimes quarrel among themselves, estimating one particular type of worship better than another. These *kaniṣṭha adhikāris*, in the lowest stage of devotion, are called materialistic devotees, or those just trying to transcend the material boundary to reach the spiritual plane.

Next above these *kaniṣṭha adhikāris* are the *madhyam adhikāris*, the devotees who are in the intermediate stage of devotional service. These *madhyam adhikāris* observe four principles in relation to the Supreme Lord, which are as follows:

1. They see, first of all, the Supreme Lord;
2. They see next the devotees of the Lord;
3. They see also the innocent, who have no knowledge about God; and at last,
4. They see the atheists who have no faith in the Lord, and who hate those in the devotional line.

The *madhyam adhikāri* devotee behaves differently toward the different above-mentioned four principles. He adores the Lord, considering Him the object of love, and he makes friendship with those who are in the devotional line. He tries to awaken the dormant love of Godhead in the hearts of the innocent people, but he does not approach the atheists who deride at the very Name of the Lord.

Above the *madhyam adhikāri* there is the *uttama adhikāri* devotee, who sees everything in relation to the Supreme Lord. He does not make any particular discrimination between the atheist and the theist, but sees in every one of them the part and parcel of God. He knows that there is no difference between a vastly learned *Brāhmaṇa* and a dog in the street, because both of them are of the Lord, though in different embodiments due to the different qualities of material action. The *Brāhmaṇa* particle of the Supreme Lord has not misused the little independence given him by the Lord, but the dog particle has misused his independence, and thus he has been punished by the law of Nature, being encaged in the ignorant form of a dog. Without considering the respective actions of the *Brāhmaṇa* and the dog, the *uttama adhikāri* tries to do good to both. Such a learned devotee of the Lord is not misled by the material bodies of the *Brāhmaṇa* and the dog, but he is attracted by the spiritual spark within the respective entities.

Those who imitate an *uttama adhikāri* in terms of the sense of oneness or fellowship, but who behave in terms of bodily relationships, are false philanthropists. Therefore the concept of universal brotherhood must be learnt from the *uttama adhikāri* devotee of the Lord, and not from a foolish person who has no proper vision of the individual soul and of the Supersoul—the plenary expansion of the Supreme Lord, Which dwells everywhere.

In this *mantra* of *Śrī Īśopaniṣad* it is clearly mentioned that one should *observe,* or see. This means one must follow the previous *ācārya,* the perfected Teacher. *Anupaśyati* is the exact Sanskrit word used in this connection. *Anu* means to observe. One should not try to see things as he does with the naked eye. The naked eye cannot see anything properly, due to its material defectiveness. One cannot see properly unless one has heard from a superior source. And the highest source is the Vedic wisdom spoken by the Lord Himself. This truth is coming in disciplic succession from the Lord to Brahmā, from Brahmā to Nārada, from Nārada to Vyāsa, and from Vyāsa to many of His disciples. Formerly there was no necessity of recording the message of the *Vedas,* because people of earlier ages were more intelligent and had sharper memories, and they could follow instructions simply by hearing once from the mouth of a bona fide spiritual master.

At present there are many commentaries on the revealed Scriptures, but most of them are not in the line of Śrīla Vyāsadeva, Who originally taught the Vedic wisdom. The final, most perfect and sublime work of Śrīla Vyāsadeva is the *Śrīmad-Bhāgavatam,* Which is the correct commentary on the *Vedānta-sūtra.* Similarly, there is the *Bhagavad-gītā,* Which is spoken by the Lord Himself and Which was recorded by Vyāsadeva. These are the more important of the many revealed Scriptures, and any commentary which does not conform to the principles of the *Gītā* or the *Śrīmad-Bhāgavatam* is unauthorized. There is complete symmetrical agreement between the *Upaniṣads, Vedānta,* the *Vedas,* the *Bhagavad-gītā* and the *Śrīmad-Bhāgavatam.* Therefore, no one should try to reach any conclusion about the *Vedas* without being instructed by members of the line of Vyāsadeva, or at least those who believe in the Personality of Godhead and His diverse energies.

Only one who is already in the liberated status, according to the *Bhagavad-gītā*, can become an *uttama adhikāri* devotee, and can see everyone or every living being as his own brother. This cannot be seen by politicians who are always after some material gain. Imitation of this liberated status is to serve the outward body (for fame, or some such reward) but is not service to the spirit soul. Such imitators have no information of the Spiritual World. The *uttama adhikāri* sees the spirit soul of an entity, and serves him as spirit, which includes matter automatically.

Mantra Seven

यस्मिन् सर्वाणि भूतान्यात्मैवाभूद् विजानतः ।
तत्र को मोहः कः शोक एकत्वमनुपश्यतः ॥ ७ ॥

yasmin sarvāṇi bhūtāny
ātmaivābhūd vijānataḥ
tatra ko mohaḥ kaḥ śoka
ekatvam anupaśyataḥ.

yasmin—in the situation; *sarvāṇi*—all; *bhūtāni*—living entities; *ātmā*—the spiritual spark; *eva*—only; *ābhūt*—becomes a fact; *vijānataḥ*—one who knows; *tatra*—therein; *kaḥ*—what; *mohaḥ*—illusion; *śokaḥ*—anxiety; *ekatvam*—of the same quality; *anupaśyataḥ*—one who sees through authority, or one who sees constantly like that.

TRANSLATION

One who always sees all living entities as spiritual sparks, in quality one with the Lord, becomes a true knower of things. What is there as illusion or anxiety for him?

PURPORT

Except for the two more advanced devotees described above, no one can correctly see the spiritual position of a living being. The living entities are qualitatively one with the Supreme Lord, as the sparks of the fire are qualitatively one with the nature of the fire. But sparks are not fire as far as quantity is concerned. The quantity of heat and light present in the fire is not equal to the quantity of heat and light in the sparks. The *Mahā-bhāgavata,* the great devotee, sees oneness in the sense that everything is the energy of the Supreme Lord. And as there is no difference between the energy and the energetic, there is the sense of oneness. Without heat and light there is no meaning of fire, and yet heat and light from the analytical point of view are different from fire. But in synthesis, heat, light, and fire are all the same one thing.

The Sanskrit words found here, *ekatvam anupaśyataḥ,* mean to see the unity of the living entities from the viewpoint of the revealed Scriptures. Every individual spark of the Supreme Whole has almost eighty per cent of the known qualities of the Whole, but they are not as good as the Supreme Lord. These qualities are present in minute quantity, as the living entity is but a minute part and parcel of the Supreme Whole. This is like the drop of water and the ocean: The quantity of salt present in the drop is never comparable to the quantity of salt present in the complete ocean. But the quality of the salt present in the drop is equal in quality, in chemical composition, with that present in the ocean.

If the individual living being were equal both in quality and in quantity, then there would be no question of the living entity's being submerged by the influence of material energy. It has already been discussed in previous *mantras* that no living being, even the powerful demigods, can surpass the Supreme Being in any respect. Therefore *ekatvam* does not mean that a living being is equal in all respects with the Supreme Lord. It means, in a broader sense, that there is one interest, just as in a family the interest of all the members is one. In a nation, although different individual citizens are there, the national interest is one. Therefore, the living entities being parts and parcels of the same Supreme family, the interest of the Supreme Being and that of the parts and parcels is not different. Every living being is the son of the Supreme Being. As it is said in the *Bhagavad-gītā,* all living creatures, including birds, reptiles, ants, aquatics, trees, and so on, all over the universe—all are emanations from the marginal potency of the Supreme Lord. And therefore all of them belong to the same family of the Supreme Being. There is no clash of interest in spiritual life.

The spiritual entities are meant for enjoyment. By nature, by constitution, every living being—both the Supreme Lord and each different part and parcel—is meant for enjoyment eternally. The living beings who are encaged in the material tabernacle are also seeking enjoyment always, but they are seeking their enjoyment on a platform which is not meant for them. Aside from this material world, there is the spiritual platform where the Supreme Being is enjoying with His innumerable associates, without any trace of material qualities. That platform is called *nirguṇa*. On the *nirguṇa* platform there is no clash of enjoyment. Here in the material world there is always a clash between different individual beings, because here the center of enjoyment is missed. The center of enjoyment is the Supreme Lord, Who is the center of the sublime and spiritual *rāsa* dance. We are all meant for joining Him, and for enjoying life with one transcendental interest and without any clash. That is the high platform of spiritual interest, and as soon as such a perfect form of oneness is realized there can be no question of illusion or lamentation.

Māyā, or illusion, means a Godless civilization, the result of which is lamentation. The Godless civilization sponsored by the modern politicians is always full of anxieties, and that is the law of Nature. No one can surpass this law, as is stated in the *Bhagavad-gītā.* Only those who surrender at the Lotus Feet of the Supreme Lord can overcome the stringent laws of Nature. If, therefore, we wish to get rid of all sorts of illusion and anxiety and create unity of all diverse interests, we must bring God into all our activities.

The results of our activities must be used to serve the interest of the Lord, and not for any other purpose, because only by serving the interest of the Lord can we feel the *ātma-bhūta* interest mentioned here in *Śrī Īśopaniṣad.* This and the *Brahmā-bhūta* interest mentioned in the *Bhagavad-gītā* are one and the same thing: The Supreme *Ātman,* or Soul, is the Lord Himself, and the minute *ātman* is the living entity. The Supreme *Atman* or *Paramātman* alone maintains all the individual minute beings, because the Supreme Lord wants to derive pleasure out of their affection. The father extends himself by his children and maintains them in order to derive pleasure. If the children of the father are obedient to his will, family affairs will run smoothly with one interest and a pleasing atmosphere. Exactly the same thing is transcendentally arranged in the *Brahman,* or Absolute family of the *Param Brahman,* the Supreme Spirit.

The *Param Brahman* is as much a Person as the individual entities are. None of them are impersonal. Such transcendental personalities are full of transcendental bliss, knowledge and life eternal. That is the real position of spiritual existence, and as soon as one is fully cognizant of this transcendental position he at once surrenders unto the Lotus Feet of the Supreme Being, *Śrī* Kṛṣṇa. But such *mahātmās,* Great Souls, are very rarely seen, because such transcendental realization is achieved only after many, many births. Once attained, however, there is no more illusion or distress, no more of the misery of material existence, and there is no birth and death as we experience in the present status of our life. That is the information we get from this *mantra* of *Śrī Īśopaniṣad.*

Mantra Eight

स पर्यगाच्छुक्रमकायमव्रण-
मस्नाविरं शुद्धमपापविद्धम् ।
कविर् मनीषी परिभूः स्वयम्भूर्
याथातथ्यतोऽर्थान् व्यदधाच्छाश्वतीभ्यः समाभ्यः ॥८॥

sa paryagāc chukram akāyam avraṇam
asnāviraṁ śuddham apāpa-viddham
kavir manīṣī paribhūḥ svayambhūr
yāthātathyato'rthān vyadadhāc chāśvatībhyaḥ samābhyaḥ.

saḥ—that person; *paryagāt*—must know in fact; *śukram*—the omnipotent; *akāyam*—unembodied; *avraṇam*—without any reproach; *asnāviram*—without any veins; *śuddham*—antiseptic; *apāpa-viddham*—prophylactic; *kaviḥ*—omniscient; *manīṣī*—philosopher; *paribhūḥ*—the greatest of all; *svayambhūḥ*—self-sufficient; *yāthātathyataḥ*—just in pursuance of; *arthān*—desirables; *vyadadhāt*—awards; *śāśvatibhyaḥ*—immemorial; *samābhyaḥ*—time.

TRANSLATION

Such a person must know in fact the Greatest of all, Who is unembodied, omniscient, beyond reproach, without veins, pure and uncontaminate, the self-sufficient Philosopher Who is awarding everyone's desire since time immemorial.

PURPORT

Here is the description of the transcendental and eternal Form of the Absolute Personality of Godhead. The Supreme Lord is not formless. He has His own transcendental Form Which is not at all similar to those of the mundane world. The living entities in this world have their forms embodied by the material Nature, and they work like any material machines. The physiological and anatomical structure of the body of a living being must have a mechanical construction, with veins and so forth in the embodiment. But in the transcendental body of the Lord there is nothing like veins. It is clearly stated here that He is unembodied. That means that there is no difference between His body and soul, nor does He accept a body by the law of Nature as we do. In the material concept of bodily life, the soul is different from the gross embodiment and subtle mind. The Supreme Lord is apart from any such compartmentalized arrangement, however. There is nothing like a difference of body and mind in the Supreme Lord. He is the Complete Whole, and His mind and body and He Himself are all one and the same.

In the *Brahma-saṁhitā* there is a similar description of the body of the Supreme Lord. He is described there as the *sac-cid-ānanda-vigraha.* This means that He is the eternal Form fully representing transcendental Existence, Knowledge and Bliss. The Vedic literature states clearly that He has a completely different kind of transcendental body, and thus He is sometimes described as formless. This formlessness means that He has no form like ours, or that He is devoid of a form which we can perceive. In the *Brahma-saṁhitā* it is further said that the Lord can do anything and everything with any one of the parts of His body. It is said there that with each and every one of the parts of His body, such as the hand, He can do the work of the other senses. This means that the Lord can walk with His hands, He can accept a thing by His legs, He can see by His hands and feet, and He can eat by His eyes. In the *Śruti mantras* it is said that He has no hands and no legs like us, but that He has a different type of hand and leg, by which He can accept all that we offer Him, and walk faster than anyone anywhere. These things are confirmed in this *mantra* of *Śrī Īśopaniṣad* by the use of words like omnipotent.

The Lord's *Śrī Vigraha,* His worshipable form, Which is installed in the temples by authorized *ācāryas* who have realized the Lord in terms of *Mantra* Seven, is also non-different from the Original Form of the Lord. The Original Form of the Lord is that of Śrī Kṛṣṇa. Śrī Kṛṣṇa expands Himself by an unlimited number of Forms like Baladeva, Rāma, Nṛsiṁha, Varāha, etc.—and all of These are one and the same Personality of Godhead.

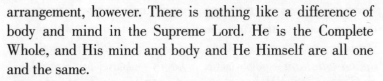

Similarly, the *Arcā-vigraha* Which is worshiped in the temples is also an expanded Form of the Lord. By worshiping the *Arcā-vigraha* of the Lord, one can at once approach the Lord, Who accepts the service of the devotee by His omnipotent energy without any reproach. The *Vigraha* of the Lord descends by request of the *ācāryas,* the holy teachers, and works exactly in the original way by His omnipotent energy.

Foolish people who have no knowledge of these *mantras* of *Śrī Īśopaniṣad,* or of any other *Śruti mantras,* consider that the *Śrī Vigraha* Who is worshiped by the pure devotees is made of material elements. To the imperfect eyes of the foolish people, or to the *kaniṣṭha adhikāris,* this Form is considered material. But such people with little knowledge do not know that the Lord, being omnipotent and omniscient, can transform matter into spirit and spirit into matter, as He desires.

In the *Bhagavad-gītā,* the Lord regrets the fallen condition of men with little knowledge, who regard the body of the Lord as material because He descends like a man into this world. Such poorly informed persons do not know the omnipotence of the Lord. To the mental speculators, therefore, the Lord does not manifest Himself in fullness. He can be appreciated only in proportion to one's surrender to Him. And the fallen condition of the living entities is due entirely to forgetfulness of our relationship with God.

In this *mantra,* as well as in many others in the *Vedas,* it is clearly mentioned: from time immemorial, the Lord is supplying. The living being first of all desires, and then the Lord supplies the object of desire in proportion to the degree of qualification. If a man wants to be a high court judge he must not only have acquired the necessary qualifications, but he must also depend upon the disposition of the authority concerned, who can award the title of high court judge. Simple acquisition of the qualifications of a high court judge is not sufficient in order to occupy the post. This must be awarded by some superior authority. Similarly, the Lord awards enjoyment to the living being in proportion to his qualifications—in other words, by the law of *karma.* Those qualifications, however, are not sufficient without the mercy of the Lord.

Ordinarily the living being does not know what to ask for from the Lord or what post to qualify himself for. When the living being knows his constitutional position, however, he asks to be accepted into the transcendental association of the Lord, in order to render transcendental loving service unto Him. Instead of asking for this, the living being under the influence of material Nature asks for many other things, and his mentality is described in the *Bhagavad-gītā* as divided, or splayed, intelligence. Spiritual intelligence is one, but the opposite number is of many varieties. In the *Śrīmad-Bhāgavatam* it is said that persons who are captivated by the temporary beauties of the external energy forget their real aim of life, which is to go back to Godhead. Forgetting this, one tries to adjust things by various plans and programs, which are compared with the process of chewing already chewed refuse. But the Lord is so kind that He allows the forgetful living being to do so without interfering in his activities. If a living being wants to go to hell, the Lord allows him to do so without interference, and if he wants to go back to home, back to Godhead, the Lord also helps him to do that.

God is described here as *paribhūḥ,* the greatest of all. No one is greater than, or equal to Him. Other living beings are described here as beggars who ask from the Lord, and the Lord supplies their desirables. If other entities were equal to the Lord in potency, or if they were omnipotent or omniscient, there would be no question of begging from the Lord even for so-called liberation. The real liberation of the living being is to go back to Godhead. Otherwise, liberation as conceived by the impersonalist remains a myth, and the begging business for sense gratification has to continue eternally, unless the beggar comes to his senses and realizes his constitutional position.

The Supreme Lord is self-sufficient. When Lord Kṛṣṇa appeared on Earth 5,000 years ago He displayed the full manifestation of Godhead by His various activities. In His childhood He killed many powerful demons, and there was no question of acquiring such power by any extraneous endeavor. He lifted Govardhana Hill without any practice of weightlifting. He danced with the *gopīs* without any social restriction, and without any reproach. Although the *gopīs* approached Him with feelings of amorous love, the mixing of the *gopīs* and Lord Kṛṣṇa has been worshiped even by Lord Caitanya, Who was a strict *sannyāsin* and rigid follower of disciplinary regulations. To confirm this, *Śrī Īśopaniṣad* says that He is "antiseptic" and "prophylactic," pure and uncontaminate. He is antiseptic in the sense that even an impure thing in the estimation of the mundane world can become purified just by touching Him. The word prophylactic refers to His association, and is mentioned in the *Bhagavad-gītā*. There it is said that a scrupulous devotee may appear in the beginning to be *durācāra*, not well-behaved. Yet he is still to be accepted as pure because he is on the right path. That is the prophylactic nature of the Lord's association.

The Lord is *apāpaviddham*, that is, nothing like sin can touch Him. Even if He may do something which appears to be sinful, such actions are all good, as there is no question of the Lord's being affected by sin. In all circumstances He is *śuddham,* most purified, often compared to the Sun. The Sun exacts moisture from many untouchable places of the earth, and itself remains pure. In fact it purifies obnoxious things by its sterilizing effect. If the Sun is so powerful, although only a material object, we can imagine the purity and strength of the All-powerful Lord.

Mantra Nine

अन्धं तमः प्रविशन्ति येऽविद्यामुपासते ।
ततो भूय इव ते तमो य उ विद्यायाꣳ रताः ॥ ९ ॥

andhaṁ tamaḥ praviśanti
ye'vidyām upāsate
tato bhūya iva te tamo
ya u vidyāyāṁ ratāḥ.

andham—gross ignorance; *tamaḥ*—darkness; *praviśanti*—enter into; *ye*—those; *avidyām*—nescience; *upāsate*—worship; *tataḥ*—further; *bhūyaḥ*—considered; *iva*—like; *te*—those; *tamaḥ*—darkness; *ye*—those; *u*—also; *vidyāyam*—in the culture of knowledge; *ratāḥ*—engaged in.

TRANSLATION

Those who are engaged in the culture of nescient activities shall enter into the darkest region of ignorance. Worse still are those engaged in the so-called culture of knowledge.

PURPORT

In this *mantra* there is a comparative study of *vidyā* and *avidyā. Avidyā,* or ignorance, is undoubtably dangerous, but *vidyā,* or knowledge, when mistaken or misguided, is even more dangerous. In modern human civilization this explanation of *Śrī Īśopaniṣad* is more applicable than at any other time in the past. Modern civilization has advanced considerably in the matter of mass education, and yet the result is that people are more unhappy than before on account of too much stress on material advancement, without any taste for the most important aspect of life, the spiritual aspect.

As far as *vidyā* is concerned, the first *mantra* of *Śrī Īśopaniṣad* has explained very clearly that the Supreme Lord is the Proprietor of everything, and forgetfulness of this fact is called ignorance. The more a man forgets this fact of life, the more he is in darkness; and in view of this, a Godless civilization directed toward the so-called advancement of education is more dangerous than a civilization in which the mass of people are less advanced.

There are different classes of men, called *karmis, jñānins* and *yogis.* The *karmis* are those who are engaged in the activities of sense gratification. Almost 99.9 per cent of the people in modern civilization are engaged in the activities of sense gratification under the flags of various activities such as industrialism, economic development, altruism, political consciousness, and so on. But all these activities are more or less based on the satisfaction of the senses, without any reference to the sort of God consciousness described in the first *mantra* of *Śrī Īśopaniṣad.*

In the language of the *Bhagavad-gītā,* people who are engaged in gross sense gratification are *mūḍhas*—in darkness like the ass, the symbol of stupidity. People who are simply engaged in the pursuit of sense gratification, without any real profit in life, are in the estimation of *Śrī Īśopaniṣad* worshiping *avidyā*. And those who play the role of helping this sort of civilization in the name of educational advancement are doing more harm than those who are on the platform of gross sense gratification. The advancement of learning by the Godless people is as dangerous as a valuable jewel on the hood of a cobra. The cobra decorated with such a valuable jewel is quite as dangerous as one which is not so decorated.

Again, the advancement of educational activities by a Godless people is, according to the *Hari-bhakti-sudhodaya*, a decoration for a dead body. In India as in many other countries, some people follow the custom of leading a procession with a decorated dead body for the pleasure of the lamenting relatives. In the same sense, modern civilization is a patchwork of activities meant to cover the perpetual miseries of material existence. Such activities are targetted toward sense gratification, but above the senses there is the mind, and above the mind there is the intelligence, and above intelligence there is the soul. Therefore, the aim of education should be self realization, realization of the spiritual values of the soul. Any education which does not lead to such a realization of life must be considered *avidyā*, or nescience. And to culture such nescience means going down to the darkest region of ignorance.

Such mistaken educators are known in the Vedic language by four names:

1. *veda-vāda-rata*,
2. *māyayā apahṛta-jñāna*,
3. *āsuraṁ bhāvam*,
4. *narādhama*.

The *veda-vāda-rata* people pose themselves as very learned in the Vedic literature, but unfortunately they are completely diverted from the purpose of the *Vedas*. In the *Bhagavad-gītā* it is said that the purpose of the *Vedas* is to know the Personality of Godhead, but these *veda-vāda-rata* men are not at all interested in the Personality of Godhead. On the contrary, they are fascinated by such results as the attainment of heaven.

As is said in *Mantra* One of *Śrī Īśopaniṣad*, we should know that the Personality of Godhead is the Proprietor of everything, and we must be satisfied with our alloted portion of the necessities of life. The purpose of the whole Vedic literature is to awaken this God consciousness in the forgetful living being, and the same principle is presented in various ways in the world's various Scriptures for the understanding of foolish mankind. Thus the ultimate purpose is to bring one back to Godhead.

But the *veda-vāda-rata* people, instead of realizing the purport of the *Vedas*, take it for granted that side issues such as the attainment of heavenly pleasure for sense gratification—the lust for which is the very cause of their material bondage in the first place—is the ultimate end of the *Vedas*. Such people misguide others by misinterpreting the Vedic literature, and sometimes they condemn the *Purāṇas*, which are authentic Vedic explanations for laymen. The *veda-vāda-ratas* make their own explanations of the *Vedas*, neglecting the authority of the great teachers, called *ācāryas;* and they tend to raise some unscrupulous person from among themselves as the leading exponent of Vedic knowledge.

These men are especially condemned by this *mantra* of *Śrī Īśopaniṣad* with the very appropriate Sanskrit word *vidyā-rata*. *Vidyā* means *Veda*, because the *Veda* is the original in all knowledge; and *rata* means engaged. *Vidyā-rata* means engaged in the study of the *Vedas*. As such, the so-called *vidyā-ratas* are condemned here because they do not know what the purpose of the *Vedas* is, on account of disobeying the *ācāryas*. Such *veda-vāda-ratas* are accustomed to finding meaning in every word of the *Vedas* to suit their own purposes. They do not know that the Vedic literature is not a collection of ordinary books and cannot be understood except through the chain of disciplic succession.

One must approach a bona fide spiritual master in order to understand the transcendental message of the *Vedas*. That is the direction of the *Kaṭha Upaniṣad*. But these *veda-vāda-rata* people have their own *ācārya*, who is not in the chain of transcendental disciplic succession. Thus they will progress into the darkest region of ignorance by misinterpreting the Vedic literature, even more so than those who have no knowledge of the *Vedas* at all.

The *māyayā apahṛta-jñāna* class of men are self-made "Gods." Such men think that they are themselves God, and there is no necessity of worshiping any other God. They will agree to worship an ordinary man if he happens to be rich, but will never worship the actual Personality of Godhead. Such foolish men cannot recognize their own foolishness, regarding the question of how God can ever have been entrapped by illusion. If God were ever entrapped by illusion, then illusion would be more powerful than God. But they also say that God is all-powerful. If God is all-powerful, then how can He be overpowered by illusion? The self-made Gods cannot answer all these questions very clearly, but they are satisfied that they have become God themselves.

Mantra Ten

अन्यदेवाहुर्विद्ययान्यदाहुरविद्यया ।
इति शुश्रुम धीराणां ये नस्तद् विचचक्षिरे ॥ १० ॥

anyad evāhur vidyayā
anyad āhur avidyayā
iti śuśruma dhīrāṇāṁ
ye nas tad vicacakṣire.

anyat—different; *eva*—certainly; *āhuḥ*—said; *vidyayā*—by culture of knowledge; *anyat*—different; *āhuḥ*—said; *avidyayā*—nescience; *iti*—thus; *śuśruma*—heard; *dhīrāṇām*—*from* the sober sect; *ye*—those; *naḥ*—to us; *tat*—that; *vicacakṣire*—explained.

TRANSLATION

The wise have explained to us that one result is derived from the culture of knowledge, and it is said that a different result is obtained from the culture of nescience.

PURPORT

The culture of knowledge can be practically conducted in the following way, as is advised in the *Bhagavad-gītā* (Thirteenth Chapter). There it is said that:

1. One should become a perfect gentleman himself, and learn to give proper respect to persons other than himself.
2. One should not pose himself as a religionist simply for name and fame.
3. One should not become a source of anxiety to others by the actions of his body, mind or words.

4. One should learn forbearance, even if there is provocation from others.
5. One should learn to avoid duplicity in his dealings with others.
6. One must have a bona fide spiritual master who can lead him gradually to the stage of spiritual realization, and to such an *ācārya* or spiritual master he must submit himself with service and relevant questions.
7. One must follow the regulative principles enjoined in the revealed Scriptures, in order to approach the platform of self realization.
8. One must be fixed up in the tenets of the revealed Scriptures.
9. One should completely refrain from practices which are detrimental to the interest of self realization.
10. One should not accept more than what he requires for the maintenance of the body.
11. One should not falsely identify himself with the material covering of the gross body nor consider as his own those who are related with his body.
12. One should always remember that so long as he has a material body, he must face the miseries of repeated birth, death, old age, and disease. There is no use in making plans to get rid of these miseries of the material body. The best thing is to find out the means by which one may regain his spiritual identity.
13. One should not be attached to more than the necessities of life required for spiritual advancement.
14. One should not be more attached to wife, children and home than is ordained in the revealed Scriptures.
15. One should not be happy or distressed in regard to the desirables and undesirables created by the mind.

16. One should become an unalloyed devotee of the Personality of Godhead, Śrī Kṛṣṇa, and serve Him with rapt attention.
17. One should develop a feeling for residing in a secluded place with a calm and quiet atmosphere favorable for spiritual culture, and thus avoid congested places where the non-devotees congregate.
18. One should become a scientist or philosopher, and make research into spiritual knowledge—not material knowledge—recognizing that spiritual knowledge is permanent, whereas material knowledge ends with the death of the body.

These eighteen items form a gradual process for developing real knowledge. Except for these eighteen items, all other items whatever are grouped within the category of nescience. Śrīla Bhaktivinode Thākur, a great *ācārya,* said that all the forms of material knowledge are merely external features of the illusory energy, and by culturing them one becomes no better than an ass. Here in *Śrī Īśopaniṣad* the same principle is repeated. Material advancement of knowledge means actually converting a human being to the status of an ass. Some materialistic politicians, under cover of spiritual garments, do decry the present system of civilization as satanic, but unfortunately they do not care for the culture of real knowledge which is described in the *Bhagavad-gītā,* and therefore they cannot change the satanic situation.

In the modern setup of things, even a boy thinks himself self-sufficient, and pays no respect to elderly men. Thus, due to the wrong type of education imparted by our universities, boys all over the world have become the cause of headache to the elderly people. Therefore *Śrī Īśopaniṣad* warns very strongly that the culture of nescience is different from that of knowledge. The universities are, so to speak, centers of nescience only, and therefore the scientists are busy discovering lethal weapons to wipe out the existence of other countries.

University students today are not given instructions on the regulative principles of *brahmacārya*, the spiritual process of life, nor do they have any faith in the respective scriptural injunctions. Religious principles are taught for the sake of name and fame only, and not for the matter of practical action. Therefore there is animosity not only in the social and political fields, but in the field of religion as well.

Nationalism in different parts of the world has also developed on account of this nescient education of the people. They have no information that this tiny earth is just a lump of matter floating in immeasurable material space along with many other lumps. In comparison to the vastness of space, these material lumps are like dust particles in the air. Because God has kindly made these lumps of matter complete in themselves, they are perfectly equipped with all necessary arrangements for floating on in space. Our sputnik drivers are very proud of their achievements, but they do not look to the Supreme Driver of these greater, more gigantic sputniks called planets.

There are innumerable suns occupying space, with innumerable arrangements of planetary systems. We small creatures, as the infinitesimal parts and parcels of the Supreme Lord, are trying to dominate these unlimited planets by repeated birth and death, but are generally frustrated by old age and disease. This span of human life is scheduled for about 100 years, although it is gradually decreasing to the limit of 20 or 30 years of life. Thanks to the culture of nescient education, befooled men have created their own nationalisms within these planets in order to grasp at sense enjoyment for these few 20 or 30 years. Such foolish people are drawing up various plans to make some demarked portion of earth as perfect as possible, which is ultimately ridiculous. And for this purpose each and every nation has become a source of anxiety for the others. More than 50% of their energy is spoiled in defense measures, with no caring for the real culture of knowledge, and they are falsely proud of becoming advanced in both material and spiritual knowledge.

Śrī Īśopaniṣad warns of this faulty mode of education, and the *Bhagavad-gītā* gives instructions as to the development of real knowledge. In this *mantra* there is a hint that the instruction of *vidyā,* knowledge, must be gained from the *dhīra. Dhīra* means undisturbed, not disturbed by material illusion. No one can be undisturbed unless and until he has perfect spiritual realization. When one is perfectly spiritually realized he has no more hankering for anything acquired, nor does he lament for anything lost. Such a *dhīra* has realized that the material body and mind which he has acquired by chance material association are foreign elements, and therefore he simply makes the best use of a bad bargain.

The material body and mind are bad bargains for the spiritual living entity. The living entity has different functions in the living world, but this material world is dead. As long as the living spiritual sparks manipulate the dead lumps of matter, the dead world appears to be a living world. But actually it is the living souls, the parts and parcels of the Supreme Living Being, which move the world. The *dhīras* are those who have come to know all these facts by hearing of them from superior authorities, and who have realized them by following the regulative principles.

To follow the regulative principles, one must go under the shelter of a bona fide spiritual master. The transcendental message comes down from the spiritual master to the disciple with the regulative principles, and not in the hazardous way of nescient education. One can become a *dhīra* only by such submissive hearing from the Personality of Godhead. The perfect disciple must be like Arjuna, and the spiritual master must be as good as the Lord Himself. These are the processes of learning *vidyā*, knowledge, from the *dhīra*, the undisturbed.

Adhīra, one who has not undergone the training of a *dhīra*, cannot be an instructive leader. Modern politicians who pose themselves as *dhīras* are themselves *adhīras*. One cannot expect perfect knowledge from them. They are busy with their own remuneration in dollars and pounds. How can they lead the mass of people to the right path of self realization? One must hear submissively from the *dhīra* in order to get actual education in life.

Mantra Eleven

विद्यां चाविद्यां च यस्तद् वेदोभयꣳ सह ।
अविद्यया मृत्युं तीर्त्वा विद्ययामृतमश्नुते ॥ ११ ॥

vidyāṁ cāvidyāṁ ca yas
tad vedobhayaṁ saha
avidyayā mṛtyuṁ tīrtvā
vidyayāmṛtam aśnute.

vidyām—knowledge in fact; *ca*—and; *avidyām*—nescience; *ca*—and; *yaḥ*—a person; *tad*—that; *veda*—knows; *ubhayam*—both; *saha*—simultaneously; *avidyayā*—by culture of nescience; *mṛtyum*—repeated death; *tīrtvā*—transcending; *vidyayā*—by culture of knowledge; *amṛtam*—deathlessness; *aśnute*—enjoys.

TRANSLATION

Only one who can learn the process of nescience and that of transcendental knowledge side by side can transcend the influence of repeated birth and death, and enjoy the full blessings of immortality.

PURPORT

Since the start of the material world everyone is trying for a permanent life, but the law of Nature is so cruel that no one has avoided the hand of death. No one wants to die. That is a practical fact. Nor does anyone want to become old or diseased. But the law of Nature does not allow anyone immunity from death, old age or disease. The advancement of material knowledge has not solved these problems of life. Material science can discover the nuclear bomb to accelerate the process of death, but it cannot discover anything which can protect man from the cruel hands of death, disease and old age.

From the *Purāṇas* we learn of the activities of Hiraṇyakaśipu: This king was materially very much advanced, and by his material acquisitions, by the strength of his nescience, he wanted to conquer death. He underwent a type of meditation so severe that all the planetary systems became disturbed by his mystic powers. He forced the creator of the universe, the demigod named Brahmā, to come down to him, and then he asked him for the benediction of becoming an *amara*, one who does not die. Brahmā refused to award this, however, because even he, the material creator, who has command over all the planets, is not himself an *amara*. He has a long duration of life, as is confirmed in the *Bhagavad-gītā*, but that does not mean that he doesn't have to die.

Hiraṇya means gold, and *kaśipu* means soft bed. This gentleman was interested in these two things, money and women, and he wanted to enjoy this sort of life by becoming artificially immortal. He asked Brahmā many things indirectly in hopes of fulfilling his desire to become an *amara*. He asked benediction that he might not be killed by any man, animal, god, or any living being within the categories of the 8,400,000 species. He also asked that he might not die on the land, in the air, in the water or by any weapon whatsoever. So on and on, Hiraṇyakaśipu thought foolishly that this would guarantee him against death. But in the end, although Brahmā granted him all these benedictions, he was killed by the Personality of Godhead in the Form of a half-man, half-lion. And no weapon was used to kill him except the nails of the Lord. He was killed on the lap of the wonderful Living Being Who was beyond his conception.

The whole point here is that even Hiraṇyakaśipu, the most powerful of materialists, could not become deathless by his various plans. What, then, will be accomplished by the tiny Hiraṇyakaśipus of today, who make plans which are throttled from moment to moment?

Śrī Īśopaniṣad instructs us not to make one-sided attempts to win the struggle for existence. Everyone is struggling hard for existence, but the law of material Nature is so hard and fast that it does not allow any to surpass it. In order to have permanent life one must be prepared to go back to Godhead.

This process of going back to Godhead is a different branch

of knowledge, and it has to be learnt from the revealed Vedic Scriptures, such as the *Upaniṣads, Vedānta, Bhagavad-gītā, Śrīmad-Bhāgavatam,* etc. Therefore, to become happy in this life and to get a permanent blissful life after leaving this material body, one must take to this sacred literature and obtain transcendental knowledge. The conditioned living being has forgotten his eternal relation with God, and he has mistakenly accepted the temporary place of birth as all-in-all. The Lord has kindly delivered the above-mentioned Scriptures in India and other Scriptures in other countries to remind the forgetful human being that his home is not here in this material world. The living being is a spiritual entity, and he can only be happy by returning to his spiritual home, with the Godhead.

The Personality of Godhead, from His Kingdom, sends His bona fide servants to propagate this mission of going back to Godhead, and sometimes He comes Himself to do this work. All living beings are His beloved sons, His parts and parcels, and therefore God is more sorry than we ourselves are for the sufferings which we are constantly undergoing in the material condition. The miseries of the material world are also indirect reminders of our incompatibility with dead matter, and intelligent living entities generally take note of these reminders, and side by side engage themselves in the culture of *vidyā,* or transcendental knowledge. Human life is the best opportunity for the culture of spiritual knowledge, and the human being who does not take advantage of this opportunity in human life is called a *narādhama,* the lowest of human beings.

The path of *avidyā,* or material advancement of knowledge for sense gratification, means repetition of death and repetition of birth also. The living entity, as he is spiritually, has no birth or death. Birth and death are concerned with the outward covering of the spirit soul, the body. This is compared with the putting on and taking off of outward garments. Foolish human beings who are grossly absorbed in the culture of *avidyā*, nescience, do not mind this cruel process, but, being enamored of the beauty of the illusory energy, they do the same things over repeatedly, without learning any lesson from the law of Nature.

The culture of *vidyā* or transcendental knowledge is essential for the human being. Unrestricted sense enjoyment in the diseased, material condition of the senses must be restricted as far as possible. Unrestricted sense enjoyment in this bodily condition is the path of ignorance and death. The living entities are not without spiritual senses. Every living being in his original spiritual form has all the senses which are now material, covered by the body and the mind. Activities of the material senses are perverted reflections of spiritual pastimes. The engagement of the spirit soul under the material covering is the diseased condition of the soul. And real sense enjoyment is possible when the disease is removed. In our pure spiritual form, freed from all material contamination, pure enjoyment of the senses is possible. The aim of human life should, therefore, not be perverted sense enjoyment, but should be to cure the material disease. Aggravating the material disease is no sign of knowledge. It is the sign of culturing *avidyā*, ignorance.

The degree of a fever must not be increased from 105 to 107 for good health. The degree is to be reduced to the normal state of 98.6. That should be the aim of human life. The modern trend of material civilization is to increase the degree of the feverish material condition, which has therefore reached the point of 107 in the form of atomic energy, with the foolish politicians crying that at any moment the world may go to hell.

That is the result of the advancement of material knowledge, and of the neglect of the most important part of life, the culture of spiritual knowledge. Here is a warning in *Śrī Īśopaniṣad* that we must not follow such a dangerous path leading to death. On the contrary, we must side by side develop the culture of spiritual knowledge so that we may become completely free from the cruel hands of death.

This does not mean that all civic activities for the maintenance of the body should be stopped. There is no question of stopping activities, as there is no question of wiping out one's temperature altogether when trying to recover from a disease. We have already tried to explain the matter by the expression "to make the best use of a bad bargain." The culture of spiritual knowledge has to be done with the help of this body and mind, and therefore maintenance of the body and mind is required if we are to reach our goal. The normal temperature should be maintained at 98.6 degrees, but it should not be foolishly increased to the degree of 107. The great sages and saints of India wanted to maintain the normal temperature by a balanced program of material and spiritual knowledge. They never allowed the misuse of human intelligence for diseased sense gratification.

Human activities diseased by a temperament of sense gratification have been regulated in the *Vedas* under the principles of Salvation. This system is found in four divisions: religion, economic development, sense gratification and salvation. At the present moment the people have no interest either in religion or salvation. They have only one aim in life, sense gratification, and in order to fulfill this end they have different plans for economic development.

Misguided man thinks that religion should be maintained for

its contribution to economic development, and that economic development is required for sense gratification. And in order to guarantee further sense gratification after death, in heaven, there is some system of religious observances. But this is not the purpose of the principles of salvation. The path of religion is actually for self realization. Economic development is required just to maintain the body in a sound, healthy condition. A man should live in a healthy condition of life with a sound mind just to realize *vidyā*, true knowledge, which is the aim of human life. This life is not meant for working like an ass or for the culture of *avidyā* or for sense gratification.

The path of *vidyā* is most perfectly presented in the *Śrīmad-Bhāgavatam*. The *Bhāgavatam* directs a human being to utilize his life in the matter of enquiring about the Absolute Truth. The Absolute Truth is realized step by step as *Brahman*, *Paramātman*, and, at last, *Bhagavān*, the Personality of Godhead. This Absolute Truth is realized by the broad-minded man who has attained knowledge and detachment, having followed the 18 principles of the *Bhagavad-gītā* described above. The central point in these 18 principles is the attainment of transcendental devotional service to the Personality of Godhead. Therefore it is recommended for all classes of men to learn the art of devotional service to the Lord.

Religiousness, economic development and sense gratification without the aim of attaining devotional service to the Lord are all different forms of nescience, as will be shown hereafter in *Śrī Īśopaniṣad*. Thus, to culture *vidyā*, especially in this age, one must always hear and chant and worship with concentrated attention, targetted on the Personality of Godhead, Who is the Lord of the transcendentalists.

Mantra Twelve

अन्धं तमः प्रविशन्ति येऽसम्भूतिमुपासते ।
ततो भूय इव ते तमो य उ सम्भूत्यां रताः ॥ १२ ॥

andhaṁ tamaḥ praviśanti
ye'sambhūtim upāsate
tato bhūya iva te tamo
ya u sambhūtyāṁ ratāḥ.

andham—ignorance; *tamaḥ*—darkness; *praviśanti*—do enter into; *ye*—those; *asambhūtim*—demigods; *upāsate*—do worship; *tataḥ*—more than that; *bhūyaḥ*—again; *iva*—like that; *te*—who; *tamaḥ*—darkness; *ye*—those; *u*—also; *sambhūtyām*—in the Absolute; *ratāḥ*—engaged.

TRANSLATION

Those who are engaged in the worship of demigods enter into the darkest region of ignorance, and still more so do the worshipers of the Absolute.

PURPORT

The Sanskrit word *asambhūti* means those who have no independent existence. *Sambhūti* is the Absolute Personality of Godhead, Who is absolutely independent of everything. In the *Bhagavad-gītā*, the Absolute Personality of Godhead, Śrī Kṛṣṇa, positively describes Himself in the following words: "I am the Supreme Cause of the powers delegated to the demigods, the great sages and the mystics. And because these are endowed with limited powers, it is very difficult for them to know how I appear Myself, by My own internal potency, in the form of a man."

All philosophers and great *ṛṣis*, or mystics, try to distinguish the Absolute from the relative by their tiny brain power. However, this can only help them to reach the point of negating relativity, without realizing any positive trace of the Absolute. Definition of the Absolute by negation is not a complete concept. Such negative definitions lead one to create a concept of his own, and one then imagines that the Absolute must be formless and without qualities. But these negations are simply the opposite numbers of the relative forms and qualities, and are themselves therefore relative. By such a concept of the Absolute one can at the utmost reach to the impersonal effulgence of God, known as *Brahman*; but one cannot make further progress to the stage of *Bhagavān*, the Personality of Godhead.

Such mental speculators do not know that Kṛṣṇa is the Absolute Personality of Godhead, and that the impersonal *Brahman* is the glaring effulgence of His transcendental body, while *Paramātman*, the Supersoul, is His all-pervading representation. They do not know that Kṛṣṇa has His eternal Form, with transcendental qualities of eternal bliss and knowledge. The dependent demigods and great sages imperfectly realize Him as one of the powerful demigods, but they consider that the *Brahman* effulgence is the ultimate Absolute Truth. Kṛṣṇa's devotees, however—who by dint of their unalloyed devotion surrender unto Him—can know that He is the Absolute Person, and that everything emanates from Him only. Such devotees continuously render loving service unto Kṛṣṇa, the Fountainhead of everything.

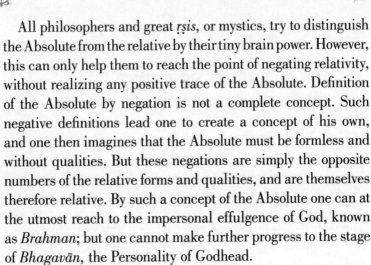

In the *Bhagavad-gītā* it is also said that only bewildered persons, driven by a strong desire for sense gratification, worship the demigods for the satisfaction of temporary problems. A temporary relief from a certain difficulty by the grace of some demigod is the demand of less intelligent persons. The living being is in the material entanglement, and he has to be relieved from material bondage entirely to obtain permanent relief on the spiritual plane, where eternal bliss, life and knowledge exist.

In the *Bhagavad-gītā* it is said that the worshipers of the demigods can go to the planets of the respective demigods. The Moon worshipers can go to the Moon, the Sun worshipers can go to the planet of the Sun, and so on. Modern scientists are now trying to go to the Moon with the help of rockets, which is not really a new attempt. The human being with his advanced consciousness is naturally inclined to travel in outer space and to reach other planets, either by sputniks, by mystic powers, or by worshiping the particular predominating deity on that planet. In the Vedic scriptures it is said that one can reach other planets in any of the ways mentioned above, most generally by worshiping the demigod presiding over the particular planet. But these planets are temporary residential places; the only permanent planets are the *Vaikuṇṭha-lokas,* found in the spiritual sky, where the Personality of Godhead predominates. The *Bhagavad-gītā* confirms this as follows:

> Even though one may rise to the highest planet, *Brahmā-loka,* one has to come back again. But if someone attains to Me (in the spiritual world), he doesn't have to take birth again.

Śrī Īśopaniṣad suggests that one remains in the darkest region by hovering over the material planets, whatever his means may be. The whole universe is covered by the gigantic material elements, just like a coconut ball half-filled with water. As it is airtight and fully covered, the darkness within is dense, and therefore planets like the Sun and the Moon are required to illuminate the inside of the universe. Outside the universe there is a vast expansion of unlimited *Brahma-jyoti* space, full of *Vaikuṇṭha-lokas*.

The biggest and the highest planet in the *Brahma-jyoti* is the *Kṛṣṇa-loka*, or *Goloka* Vṛndāvana, where the Personality of Godhead, Śrī Kṛṣṇa, resides. Lord Śrī Kṛṣṇa never quits this *Kṛṣṇa-loka* where He dwells with His eternal associates, and yet He is omnipresent throughout the complete material and spiritual cosmic situation. This fact has already been explained in *Mantra* Four of *Śrī Īśopaniṣad*. The Lord is present everywhere, as the Sun is. A man can move through space with the highest possible speed, and still he will find that the Sun is there, although the Sun is situated in its own undeviating orbit.

The problem of life cannot be solved by going to the Moon. There are many pseudo-worshipers who become religionists for the sake of name and fame only. Such pseudo-religionists do not wish to get out of this universe and reach the spiritual sky. They want only to maintain the status quo in the material world, under the garb of worshiping the Lord. And the atheists and the impersonalists lead such foolish pseudo-religionists into the darkest regions by preaching the cult of atheism. The atheist directly denies the existence of the Supreme Personality of Godhead, and the impersonalist supports the atheist by preaching the impersonal existence of the Supreme Lord. As far as we have gone through *Śrī Īśopaniṣad*, we have not come across any *mantra* where the Personality of Godhead is denied. It is said that He can run faster than anyone. Those who are running after the planets are certainly persons, and if the Lord can run faster than all of them, why should He be considered impersonal? The impersonal conception of the Supreme Lord is another face of ignorance, due to an imperfect vision of the Absolute Truth.

And so the ignorant pseudo-religionists, the manufacturers of so-called incarnations—directly violating the Vedic injunctions—are liable to enter into the darkest region of the universe, on account of their business of misleading those who follow them. These impersonalists generally pose themselves as incarnations of God to the foolish, who have no knowledge of the Vedic wisdom. And if such foolish men have any knowledge at all, it is more dangerous in their hands than ignorance itself. Such impersonalists do not even worship the demigods as is recommended in the scriptures.

In the scriptures there is a recommendation for worshiping the demigods under different circumstances, but at the same time it is said that there is no real need for this. In the *Bhagavad-gītā* it is clearly stated that the results of worshiping the demigods are not permanent. The whole material world is not permanent, and therefore anything achieved here within the darkness of material existence is also impermanent. The problem, then, is how to obtain real and permanent life.

The Lord states that as soon as one reaches Him by devotional service—which is the one and only way to approach the Personality of Godhead—there is complete freedom from the bondage of birth and death. In other words, the path of salvation, or getting out of the material clutches, fully depends on the principles of knowledge and detachment. And the pseudo-religionists have neither knowledge nor detachment from material affairs. Most of them want to continue in the golden shackles of material bondage, under the shadow of altruistic and philanthropic activities, and in the name of religious principles. By false religious sentiments they present a make-show of devotional service, indulging in all sorts of immoral principles, and still pass as spiritual masters and devotees of God. Such violators of religious principles have no respect for the authoritative *ācāryas*, the holy teachers in the strict disciplic succession; and to mislead the people in general they themselves become so-called *ācāryas*, without even following the principles of the *ācāryas*.

These rogues in human society are the most dangerous elements and, for want of religious government, they pass on without being punished by the law of the state. They cannot, however, avoid the law of the Supreme, Who has clearly declared in the *Bhagavad-gītā* that these envious demons, in the garb of religious propagandists, shall be thrown down into the darkest region of hell. It is confirmed in *Śrī Īśopaniṣad* that the pseudo-religionists are heading toward the most obnoxious place in the universe after finishing with the spiritual mastership business, which is simply for the matter of sense gratification.

Mantra Thirteen

अन्यदेवाहुः सम्भवादन्यदाहुरसम्भवात् ।
इतिशुश्रुम धीराणां ये नस्तद्विचचक्षिरे ॥ १३ ॥

anyad evāhuḥ sambhavād
anyad āhur asambhavāt
iti śuśruma dhīrāṇāṁ
ye nas tad vicacakṣire.

anyat—different; *eva*—certainly; *āhuḥ*—it is said; *sambhavāt*—by worshiping the Supreme Lord, the Cause of all causes; *anyat*—different; *āhuḥ*—it is said; *asambhavāt*—by worshiping what is not the Supreme; *iti*—thus; *śuśruma*—I heard it; *dhīrāṇām*—from the undisturbed authorities; *ye*—those; *naḥ*—unto us; *tat*—about that subject matter; *vicacakṣire*—perfectly explained.

TRANSLATION

It is said that one result is obtained by worshiping the Supreme Cause of all causes, and that another is obtained by worshiping what is not supreme. All this was heard from the undisturbed authorities who clearly explained it.

PURPORT

In this *mantra* of *Śrī Īśopaniṣad* the system of hearing from the undisturbed authorities is confirmed. Unless one hears from the bona fide *ācārya,* who is never disturbed by the changes of the material world, one cannot have the real key to transcendental knowledge. The bona fide spiritual master, who has also heard the *Śruti mantras,* or Vedic knowledge, from his undisturbed *ācārya,* never manufactures or presents anything which is not mentioned in the Vedic literature. In the *Bhagavad-gītā* it is clearly said that the worshipers of the *Pitṛs,* or forefathers, reach the forefathers, the gross materialists who make plans to remain here in this world remain here, and the devotees of the Lord, who worship none but Lord Kṛṣṇa, the Supreme Cause of all causes, reach Him in His Abode in the spiritual sky.

Here also in *Śrī Īśopaniṣad,* it is said that different results are achieved by different modes of worship. If we worship the Supreme Lord, certainly we will reach the Supreme Lord in

His eternal Abode, and if we worship demigods like the Sun and Moon, we can reach these respective planets without any doubt. And if we want to remain here on this wretched planet with our planning commissions and our stop-gap political adjustments, we can certainly do that also.

Nowhere in authentic scriptures is it said that whatever you do and whatever you worship you will ultimately reach the same goal. Such foolish theories are offered by self-made masters who have no connection with the *paramparā*, the bona fide system of disciplic succession. The bona fide spiritual master cannot say that for everyone who has his own mode of worship—be it worship of the demigods or of the Supreme—it leads to the same goal. For a common man it is very easy to understand that a person starting by train from Bombay can reach the destination for which he has purchased his ticket, and nowhere else. A person who has purchased a ticket for Calcutta can reach Calcutta. But contemporary so-called masters preach that, whatever spiritual ticket you may purchase, it will take you to the Supreme Goal. Such mundane and compromising offers attract many foolish creatures to become puffed up with their manufactured methods of spiritual realization, but the Vedic instruction doesn't uphold them. Unless one has received knowledge from the bona fide spiritual master—one who is in the recognized line of disciplic succession—one cannot have the real thing as it is. The *Bhagavad-gītā* says:

> Thus, O chastiser of the foe, the *yoga* principles [of the *Gītā*] were known to the great kings. But, the *paramparā* system being broken, these principles appear now to be lost.

When Lord Śrī Kṛṣṇa was present in this world, the *bhakti-yoga* principles defined in the *Bhagavad-gītā* had become distorted, and so the Lord had to re-establish the disciplic system, beginning with Arjuna, who was the most confidential friend and devotee of the Lord. The Lord clearly said to Arjuna that it was because he was His devotee and friend that the principles of the *Gītā* were understandable to him. In other words, no one can understand the *Gītā* who is not a devotee and friend of the Lord. This means that only one who follows the path of Arjuna can understand the *Gītā.*

At the present moment there are many interpreters of this sublime dialogue who have nothing to do with Arjuna or Lord Kṛṣṇa. They interpret the verses of the *Bhagavad-gītā* in their own ways, and postulate all sorts of rubbish in the name of the *Gītā.* Such interpreters believe neither in Śrī Kṛṣṇa nor in His eternal Abode. So, then, what can they explain about the *Bhagavad-gītā?*

The *Gītā* clearly says that only those who have lost their senses worship the demigods. Kṛṣṇa ultimately advises that one should give up all other ways and modes of worship, and fully surrender unto Him only. Those persons who are cleansed of all sinful reactions can have such unflinching faith in the Supreme Lord. Others will continue hovering over the material sphere with their paltry ways of worship, and thus will be misled from the real path, under the false impression that all paths lead to the same goal.

In this *mantra* the Sanskrit word *sambhavāt,* worship of the Supreme Cause, is very significant. Lord Kṛṣṇa is the Original Personality of Godhead, and everything that exists has emanated from Him. In the *Gītā* the Lord explains Himself. He says there that He is the Creator of everyone, including Brahmā, Viṣṇu and Śiva. And because these three principal deities of the material world are created by the Lord, He is the

Creator of all that exists in the material and spiritual worlds.

In the *Atharva Veda* it is similarly said that One Who existed before the creation of Brahmā and One Who enlightened Brahmā with Vedic knowledge is Lord Srī Kṛṣṇa. "The Supreme Person desired to create the living entities, and thus Nārāyaṇa created all the beings. From Nārāyaṇa, Brahmā was born. Nārāyaṇa created all the *Prajāpatis.* Nārāyaṇa created Indra. Nārāyaṇa created the eight Vasus. Nārāyaṇa created the eleven Rudras. Nārāyaṇa created the twelve Ādityas." This Nārāyaṇa being the plenary manifestation of Lord Kṛṣṇa, Nārāyaṇa and Kṛṣṇa are one and the same.

There are later readings also which say that the same Supreme Lord is the Son of Devakī. His childhood with Devakī and Vasudeva and His identity with Nārāyaṇa have also been confirmed by Śrīpad Śaṅkarācārya, even though Śaṅkara does not belong to the Vaiṣṇava, or personalist, cult. There are still other readings, also in the *Atharva Veda,* such as this: "Only Nārāyaṇa existed in the beginning, and there was no existence of Brahmā or Śiva, nor of Agni, the fire, nor of water. There were no stars, there was no Sun, no Moon. He does not remain alone. He creates as He desires."

In the *Mokṣa-dharma* it is said: "I created the Prajāpatis and the Rudras. They have not complete knowledge of Me because they are also covered by My illusory energy."

In the *Varāha Purāṇa* it is said: "Nārāyaṇa is the Supreme Personality of Godhead, and from Him the four-headed Brahmā became manifested, as also did Rudra, who later became omniscient."

Thus all Vedic literature will confirm this view that Nārāyaṇa or Kṛṣṇa is the Cause of all causes. In the *Brahma-saṁhitā* also it is said that the Supreme Lord is Śrī Kṛṣṇa. He is "Govinda", the Delighter of every living being, and He is the Primeval Cause of all causes. The really learned person will know all this by the evidence of great sages and the *Vedas*, and will thus decide to worship Lord Kṛṣṇa as all-in-all.

Persons are called *buddha*, or really learned, who fasten themselves only to the worship of Śrī Kṛṣṇa. This conviction can be established when one hears the transcendental message from the undisturbed *ācārya*, with faith and love. One who has no faith in, or love for, Lord Kṛṣṇa cannot be convinced of this simple truth. Such faithless persons are described in the *Bhagavad-gītā* as *mūdhas*, foolish as the ass. It is said that the *mūdhas* deride the Personality of Godhead because they don't have complete knowledge from the undisturbed *ācārya*. One who is disturbed by the whirlpool movements of the material energy is not qualified to become an *ācārya*.

Before hearing the *Gītā*, Arjuna was disturbed by this whirlpool—the reaction of family, society and community affection—and thus he wanted to become a philanthropist and a nonviolent man of the world. But when he became *buddha*, by hearing the Vedic knowledge of the *Bhagavad-gītā* from the Supreme Person, he changed his decision and became a worshiper of Lord Śrī Kṛṣṇa, Who had Himself designed the Battle of Kurukṣetra. Arjuna worshiped the Lord by fighting with his so-called relatives, and thus became a pure devotee of the Lord. Such achievements are possible only by worshiping the real Kṛṣṇa and not by worshiping some fabricated "Kṛṣṇa" inaugurated by foolish men who are without knowledge of the intricacies of the science of Kṛṣṇa described in the *Gītā* and in the *Śrīmad-Bhāgavatam*.

According to the *Vedānta-sūtra*, the *Sambhūta* is the source of birth and sustenance, and the reservoir after annihilation.

The *Śrīmad-Bhāgavatam,* the natural commentary upon the *Vedānta-sūtras* by the same author, comments that the source of all emanations is not a dead stone, but is *abhijñaḥ,* or fully conscious. Therefore, the Primeval Lord Śrī Kṛṣṇa says in the *Gītā* that He is fully conscious of the past, the present and the future; and no one, including demigods such as Śiva and Brahmā, knows Him fully. Those who are disturbed by the tides of material existence cannot know Him fully. Such half-educated spiritual masters try to make some compromise, and make the mass of human beings the object of worship. They do not know that such worship of the masses is not possible, nor are the masses perfect. This is something like pouring water on the leaves of the tree, instead of watering the root. The natural process of worship is to pour water on the root of the tree from which the leaves grow. But today's disturbed leaders become more attracted by the leaves than the root, and therefore, in spite of perpetually watering the leaves, all is drying up for want of nourishment.

Śrī Īśopaniṣad advises us to pour water on the root, the Source of all germination. Worshiping the mass population by rendering bodily service which can never be perfect is less important than service to the soul. The soul is the root generating different types of bodies in terms of the law of *karma,* or material reaction. To serve only the human being by medical aids, social amenities and educational facilities, while cutting the throats of poor animals in slaughterhouses, does not add up to any valid service to the living beings.

The living being is perpetually suffering from the material disease of birth, death, old age and disease, in different types of body. The human form of life is a chance to get out of this entanglement of material existence. This can be done simply by re-establishing the lost relationship of the living entity with the Supreme Lord. And the Lord comes personally to teach us this philosophy of surrender unto the Supreme, the *Sambhūtam*. Real service to humankind is to teach surrender unto the Supreme Lord, and to worship Him only, with full love and energy. That is the instruction of *Śrī Īśopaniṣad* in this *mantra*.

The simple way to worship the Supreme Lord in this age of disturbance is to hear and chant about His great activities. The mental speculators, however, think of the activities of the Lord as imaginary, and therefore they refrain from any such hearing process, and invent some jugglery of words, without any substance, to divert the attention of the poor innocent mass of people. Instead of hearing the activities of Lord Kṛṣṇa, they prefer to advertise themselves by inducing their followers to sing about the pseudo-spiritual master. In modern times, the number of such pretenders has increased in considerable numbers, and it has become a problem for the pure devotees of the Lord to save the mass of people from the unholy propaganda of these pretenders and imitation incarnations of God.

The *Upaniṣads* indirectly draw our attention to the Primeval Lord Śrī Kṛṣṇa, and the *Bhagavad-gītā*, which is the summary of all *Upaniṣads*, directly points out Śrī Kṛṣṇa. One should, therefore, hear about Kṛṣṇa as He is in the *Gītā* or in the *Śrīmad-Bhāgavatam*, and that will gradually help him in cleansing his mind of all contaminated things. The *Bhāgavatam* says: "By hearing the activities of the Lord, one draws the attention of the Lord towards the devotee. And the Lord, being situated in the heart of every living being, helps the devotee by giving him proper direction." The *Bhagavad-gītā* also confirms this.

This inner direction by the Lord cleanses the heart of the

devotee of all dirty things which are produced by the material modes of passion and ignorance. The non-devotees are under the direction of passion and ignorance. By passion one cannot become detached from material affinity, and by ignorance one cannot know what he actually is, and what the Lord is. Thus, in the state of passion, there is no chance for self realization however much one may play the false part of a religionist. For a devotee, by the grace of the Lord, the modes of passion and ignorance are removed, and he at once becomes situated in the quality of goodness, the sign of a perfect *Brāhmaṇa.* This stage of brāhminical qualification can be earned by anyone and everyone, provided he follows the path of devotional service under the guidance of a bona fide spiritual master. The *Bhāgavatam* says that any lowborn living entity can be made purified under the guidance of a pure devotee of the Lord, because the Lord is so extraordinarily powerful.

The first sign of brāhminical qualification is that the candidate becomes happy, and becomes enthusiastic in the matter of devotional service to the Lord. This unveils before him, automatically, all about the science of God. And, thus knowing the science of God, he gradually becomes loosened from his material attachments, and his doubtful mind becomes crystal clear, by the grace of the Lord. In this stage only can one become a liberated soul, and see the Lord in every step of life. That is the perfection of *sambhavāt,* as described in this *mantra* of *Śrī Iśopaniṣad.*

Mantra Fourteen

सम्भूतिं च विनाशं च यस्तद् वेदोभयꣳ सह ।
विनाशेन मृत्युं तीर्त्वा सम्भूत्यामृतमश्नुते ॥ १४ ॥

sambhūtiṁ ca vināśaṁ ca
yas tad vedobhyaṁ saha
vināśena mṛtyuṁ tīrtvā
sambhūtyāmṛtam aśnute.

sambhūtim—the eternal Personality of Godhead, His transcendental Name, Form, Pastimes, Qualities, Paraphernalia, and the variegatedness of His abode, etc; *ca*—and; *vināśam*—and the temporary material manifestation of demigods, man, animals, etc., along with their false name, fame, etc.; *ca*—also; *yaḥ*—as they are; *tad*—that; *veda*—knows; *ubhayam*—both; *saha*—along with; *vināśena*—everything liable to be vanquished; *mṛtyum*—death; *tīrtvā*—surpassing; *sambhūtyā*—in the eternal Kingdom of God; *amṛtam*—deathlessness; *aśnute*—enjoys.

TRANSLATION

One should know perfectly well about the Personality of Godhead and His transcendental Name, as well as the temporary material creation with its temporary demigods, men and animals. When one knows these, he surpasses death, and the ephemeral cosmic manifestation with it, and in the eternal Kingdom of God he enjoys his eternal life of bliss and knowledge.

PURPORT

Human civilization, by its so-called advancement of knowledge, has created many material things, including space capsules and atomic energy. But it has failed to create a situation in which man need not die, take his birth again, become old, or suffer from diseases. Whenever these questions are raised by an intelligent man before a so-called scientist, the scientist very cleverly replies that material science is progressing, and that it will ultimately be possible to render man deathless and ageless. Such answers by material scientists prove their gross ignorance of material Nature. In material Nature everything is under the stringent laws of matter, and must pass through six stages of existence: birth, growth, duration of life, transformation, deterioration, and death at last. Nothing that is in contact with material Nature can be beyond the above-mentioned six laws of existence, and therefore no one, whether demigod, man, animal, or tree, can survive forever here in the material world.

The duration of life may vary in different species. Lord Brahmā, the chief living being within this material world, may continue his life for millions and millions of years, while the minute germs may live just for some hours; that does not matter. No one in this material world can survive eternally. Things here are born or created under certain conditions, they stay for some time, and, if they have life then they grow, create generations, then dwindle gradually, and at last are annihilated. By that law even the Brahmās (there are millions of Brahmās in different universes—each one bigger than the last) are all liable to death, either today or tomorrow. Therefore, the whole material world is called *Martya-loka,* the place of death.

The material scientists and politicians are trying to make this place deathless because they have no information of the deathless spiritual nature, due to their ignorance of the Vedic literature. The Vedic literature is full of knowledge matured by experience. But modern man is averse to receive knowledge from the *Vedas, Purāṇas,* and other scriptures.

In the *Viṣṇu Purāṇa* we have information that Lord Viṣṇu, the Personality of Godhead, possesses different energies, known as *parā,* superior, and *aparā,* or *avidyā*—inferior. The material energy in which we are at present involved is called the *avidyā,* inferior, energy; and the material creation is made possible by such energy. But there is another, superior energy called the *parā-śakti,* where everything is different from this material inferior Nature. That nature is the eternal or deathless creation of the Lord.

All the material planets—upper, lower and intermediate, including the Sun, Moon and Venus—are scattered over the universe. These planets exist only during the lifetime of Brahmā. Some lower planets, however, are vanquished after the end of one day of Brahmā, and they are again recreated during the next daytime of Brahmā. Time calculation on the upper planets is different from that of ours. One of our years is equal to twenty-four hours, or one day and night, on many of the upper planets. The four ages of Earth *(Satya, Tretā, Dvāpara, Kali)* make a duration of twenty-two thousand years and five months in terms of the time of these upper planets. Such a length of time multiplied by one thousand is one day of Brahmā, and one night of Brahmā is the same. With such days and nights accumulating into months and years, Brahmā's life is estimated at one hundred years. And at the end of his life, the complete universal manifestation becomes vanquished.

The living beings residing in the Sun and Moon, as well as those in the *Martya-loka* system—which includes this Earth and many planets below the Earth—are all merged into devastating water during the nighttime of Brahmā. During this time no living beings or species of life remain manifested, although spiritually they continue to exist. This non-manifested stage is called *avyakta.* And again, when the entire universe is vanquished at the end of Brahmā's lifetime, there is an *avyakta* state. But beyond these two non-manifested states there is another, spiritual atmosphere or nature, where there is a great number of spiritual planets, existing eternally even when all the planets within this material universe are vanquished.

The cosmic manifestation within the jurisdiction of the various Brahmās is a display of one-fourth the energy of the Lord, and this energy is called inferior. The spiritual nature beyond the jurisdiction of Brahmā is called *tri-pada-vibhūti,* three-fourths the energy of the Lord, and is the superior energy, or *parā-prakṛti.*

The predominating Supreme Person in the spiritual nature is Lord Śrī Kṛṣṇa. He can be approached only by unqualified devotional service, and not by anything else, such as the processes of *jñāna* (philosophy) and *yoga* (mysticism), much less that of *karma* (fruitive work). The *karmis,* or fruitive workers, can elevate themselves to the *Svarga-loka* planets, including the Sun and the Moon. *Jñānins* and *yogis* can reach still higher planets, such as the *Brahmā-loka;* and, becoming still more qualified by devotional service, they are allowed to enter into the spiritual nature, either in the illuminating cosmic atmosphere of the spiritual sky (the *Brahman),* or on the planets, according to qualification. It is certain, however, that no one can enter into the spiritual planets called *Vaikuṇṭhas* without being trained in devotional service.

On the material planets, everyone from Brahmā down to the ant is trying to lord it over material Nature, and this is called the material disease. As long as this material disease continues, the living entity has to undergo the process of changing bodies, whether in the form of a demigod, a man, or an animal; and ultimately he has to endure the unmanifested condition during the two kinds of devastations: the night of Brahmā, and at the end of Brahmā's life. If we want to cease the process of repeated birth and death, and the concomitant factors of old age and disease, then we must try to enter into the spiritual planets, and Lord Kṛṣṇa by His plenary expansions is the dominating Figure on each and every one of them.

No one can predominate over Kṛṣṇa. And anyone trying to predominate over material Nature is called a conditioned soul, being subject to the laws of material Nature, suffering the pangs of repeated birth and death. The Lord comes here to reestablish the principles of religion, and the basic principle is to develop the attitude of surrender toward Him. The Lord teaches this in the last portion of the *Bhagavad-gītā*, but foolish men have tactfully misinterpreted this prime teaching, and have misled the people in diverse ways. They have been urged to open hospitals, but are not interested in educating themselves to enter into the spiritual kingdom by devotional service. They have been taught to take interest only in temporary relief work, which can never bring about real happiness for the living entity. They start varieties of public and semi-governmental institutions for tackling the devastating power of Nature. But they don't know how to pacify insurmountable Nature.

Many men are advertised as great scholars of the *Bhagavad-gītā*, but they overlook the factual method presented there to pacify material Nature. Powerful Nature can only be pacified by the awakening of God consciousness, as is clearly mentioned in the *Gītā*.

Śrī Īśopaniṣad, however, teaches in this *mantra* that one must know both the *sambhūti* and the *vināśa* perfectly, side by side. By knowing the *vināśa* alone—the temporary material manifestation—you cannot save anything: In the course of Nature, there is devastation at every moment. No one can be saved from these devastations by any efforts of hospital-opening. They can be saved only by complete knowledge of the eternal life of bliss and awareness. The whole Vedic scheme is meant to educate men in this art of achieving eternal life. People are often misguided by other, temporarily attractive things based on sense gratification, but that sort of service which thus misleads them is most degraded.

You must save your fellow man in the right sense. There is no question of liking or disliking the truth. It is there. If you want to be saved from repeated birth and death you must take to the devotional service of the Lord. There can be no compromise in the matter of necessity.

Mantra Fifteen

हिरण्मयेन पात्रेण सत्यस्यापिहितं मुखम् ।
तत् त्वं पूषन्नपावृणु सत्यधर्माय दृष्टये ॥ १५ ॥

hiraṇmayena pātreṇa
satyasyāpihitaṁ mukham
tat tvaṁ pūṣann apāvṛṇu
satya-dharmāya dṛṣṭaye.

hiraṇmayena—by effulgence of light; *pātreṇa*—by dazzling covering; *satyasya*—of the Supreme Truth; *apihitam*—covered; *mukham*—the face; *tat*—that covering; *tvam*—your Self; *pūṣan*—O the Sustainer; *apāvṛṇu*—kindly remove; *satya*—pure; *dharmāya*—unto the devotee; *dṛṣṭaye*—for exhibiting.

TRANSLATION

O my Lord, Sustainer of all that lives, Your real face is covered by Your dazzling effulgence. Kindly remove that covering and exhibit Yourself to Your pure devotee.

PURPORT

In the *Bhagavad-gītā,* the Lord explains about His Personal rays, called *Brahma-jyoti*—the dazzling effulgence of His Personal Form—as follows:

> I am the basis of the impersonal *Brahman,* which is immortal and imperishable, eternal, the constitutional position of ultimate happiness. (*Gītā,* 14/27)

Brahman, Paramātman and *Bhagavān* are three angles of vision of the same Absolute Truth. *Brahman* is the phase of the Absolute Truth most perceptible to the beginner. *Paramātman* is the phase of the Absolute Truth for those who have progressed. And *Bhagavān* is the ultimate realization of the Absolute Truth. This is confirmed in the *Gītā,* where the Lord says that He is the ultimate concept of the Absolute Truth. He is the source of *Brahma-jyoti,* as well as of the all-pervading *Paramātman* feature.

As He says that He is the ultimate reservoir of the *Brahma-jyoti,* or impersonal conception of the Absolute Truth, so also He says in the *Gītā* that there is no need of explaining His unlimited potency: it can be summarized in short that, by His one plenary portion—the all-pervading *Paramātman*—He maintains the complete material cosmic creation. And in the Spiritual World also He maintains all manifestations. Therefore, in the *Śruti mantra* of *Śrī Īśopaniṣad,* He is addressed as *Pūṣan,* the ultimate Maintainer.

The Personality of Godhead, Śrī Kṛṣṇa, is always full with transcendental bliss. When He was present at Vṛndāvana in India 5,000 years ago, He always remained in transcendental bliss, even from the beginning of His childhood pastimes. The killing of varieties of demons, such as Agha, Baka, Pūtanā and Pralamba were also pleasure excursions for Him. When He was within His village He was enjoying with His mother, sisters and friends as the naughty Butter Thief, and everyone of His associates was enjoying celestial bliss by His stealing. The Lord is known as the Butter Thief, but the term is never used in a derogatory sense. The term Butter Thief, in the case of the Lord, is used with the understanding of the pleasure of His pure devotees. Everything that was done by the Lord at Vṛndāvana was for the pleasure of His associates there. Such manifestations were created by Him to attract the dry speculators in the transcendental line, as well as the acrobats of the so-called *haṭha-yoga* system, trying to find the Absolute Truth.

Of the childhood play of the Lord with His playmates, the cowherd boys, Śukadeva Gosvāmī in the *Śrīmad-Bhāgavatam* said:

> The Personality of Godhead, Who is perceived as the impersonal *Brahman* of bliss, Who is worshiped as the Supreme Lord by the devotees, and Who is considered an ordinary human being by the mundane, played with the cowherd boys who had achieved that position after a huge accumulation of pious deeds.

Thus the Lord is ever engaged in transcendental loving activities along with His spiritual associates in the various relationships of *śānta,* calmness, *dāsya,* servitorship, *sākhya,* friendship, *vātsālya,* paternal affection, and *mādhurya,* conjugal love.

It is said that the Lord never goes out of the *Vṛndāvana-dhāma,* and so it may be asked how He manages the affairs of His different creations. This is answered in the *Gītā:* He pervades all the material creation by His plenary part, known as the *Puruṣa* incarnation. The Lord has nothing to do with material creation, maintenance and destruction, but He causes it to be done by His plenary expansion, this *Paramātman* or Supersoul feature. Every living entity is known as *ātman,* soul. The principal *Ātman,* Who controls them all, is *Paramātman*—Supersoul.

The whole system of God realization is a great science. The materialists can only analyze and meditate on the twenty-four factors of the material creation. They have very little information of the *Puruṣa*, the Lord. The impersonal transcendentalists are simply bewildered by the glaring effulgence of the *Brahma-jyoti*. If one wants to see the Absolute Truth in full, one has to penetrate beyond the twenty-four material elements and the glaring effulgence as well. *Sri Īśopaniṣad* hints at this direction, praying for removal of the *hiraṇmaya-pātra*, the dazzling covering. Unless this covering is removed, and unless one can perceive the Supreme Personality of Godhead as He is, factual realization of the Absolute Truth can never be achieved.

The *Paramātman* feature of the Personality of Godhead is one of three plenary expansions, collectively called *Viṣṇu-tattva*. The *Visnu-tattva* within the universe (one of the three principal deities—Brahmā, Viṣṇu and Śiva) is known as the *Kṣirodaka-śāyī Viṣṇu*. He is the all-pervading *Paramātman* in each and every individual living entity. And the *Garbhodaka-śāyī Viṣṇu* is the collective Supersoul of all living entities. Beyond these two there is the *Kāraṇodaka-śāyī Viṣṇu* lying in the Causal Ocean. He is the Creator of all the universes. The *yoga* system teaches the serious student to meet such *Viṣṇu-tattvas* after overcoming the twenty-four material elements of cosmic creation. The culture of empiric philosophy helps one to realize the impersonal *Brahma-jyoti*, which is the glaring effulgence of the transcendental body of Lord Śrī Kṛṣṇa. This is confirmed in the *Bhagavad-gītā* as well as in the *Brahma-saṁhitā* (5/40):

> In the millions and millions of universes, there are innumerable planets, each and every one of them different from the others by cosmic constitution, and all of them situated in a corner of the *Brahma-jyoti*. This *Brahma-jyoti* is the Personal ray of the Supreme Personality of Godhead, Whom I do worship.

This *mantra* of the *Brahma-saṁhitā* is the position of factual realization of the Absolute Truth, and the *Śruti mantra* of *Sri Īśopaniṣad* under discussion is a confirmation of this *mantra* as a process of realization. It is a simple prayer to the Lord to remove the *Brahma-jyoti,* so that one can see the real face of God.

Perfect knowledge means to know the root of *Brahman.* The root of *Brahman* is Lord Śrī Kṛṣṇa, and in scriptures such as the *Śrīmad-Bhāgavatam* the science of Kṛṣṇa is perfectly elaborated. In the *Bhāgavatam,* the author, Śrīla Vyāsadeva, has established by realization that the Supreme Truth is described either as *Brahman, Paramātman* or *Bhagavān.* But he has never said that the Supreme Truth is anywhere described as *jīva,* the ordinary living entity. Therefore the living entity is not the all-powerful Supreme Truth. Otherwise, there would be no need of prayer by the entity for the Lord to remove the dazzling cover in order to see His real face.

The conclusion is, therefore, that in the absence of potent manifestations of the Supreme Truth, the impersonal *Brahman* is realized. Similarly, when there is realization of the material potencies of the Lord, with little or no information of the spiritual potency, it is called *Paramātman* realization. Therefore, both *Brahman* and *Paramātman* realization of the Absolute Truth are partial realizations. But when one realizes the Supreme Personality of Godhead, Śrī Kṛṣṇa, in full potency after the removal of the *hiraṇmaya-pātra,* as is prayed for in this *mantra,* then he realizes that *Vāsudevaḥ sarvam iti:* Lord Śrī Kṛṣṇa, known as Vāsudeva, is everything—*Brahman, Paramātman* and *Bhagavān.* He is *Bhagavān,* the root, and *Brahman* and *Paramātman* are His branches.

In the *Bhagavad-gītā* there is a comparative analysis of

the three grades of transcendentalists, known as *jñānins,* the worshipers of the impersonal *Brahman,* the *yogis,* or worshipers of the *Paramātman* feature, and *bhaktas,* or devotees of Lord Śrī Kṛṣṇa. It is stated in the *Gītā* that amongst all types of transcendentalists, one who is a *jñāni,* who has cultured the Vedic knowledge, is supreme. Yet the *yogis* are still more than the *jñānins.* The *yogis* are far superior to fruitive workers as well. And amongst all kinds of *yogis,* "the one who constantly serves the Lord with all his energy is topmost."

The summary is that a philosopher is better than a laboring man, and a mystic is far superior to a philosopher. And of all the mystic *yogis,* one who is following *bhakti-yoga,* who is constantly engaged in the service of the Lord, is the highest. *Śrī Īśopaniṣad* directs us toward this perfection of life.

Mantra Sixteen

पूषन्नेकर्षे यम सूर्य प्राजापत्य
व्यूह रश्मीन् समूह ।
तेजो यत् ते रूपं कल्याणतमं
तत् ते पश्यामि योऽसावसौ पुरुषः सोऽहमस्मि ॥ १६ ॥

pūṣann ekarṣe yama sūrya prājāpatya
vyūha raśmīn samūha tejaḥ
yatte rūpaṁ kalyāṇatamaṁ tatte paśyāmi
yo 'sāvasau puruṣaḥ so 'hamasmi.

pūṣan—the Maintainer; *ekarṣe*—the primeval Philosopher; *yama*—the regulating principal; *sūrya*—the destination of the *Sūris* (great devotees); *prājāpatya*—the well-wisher of the *Prajāpatis* (progenitors of Mankind); *vyūha*—kindly arrange; *raśmīn*—the rays; *samūha*—wind up; *tejaḥ*—effulgence; *tat*—that; *te*—your; *rūpam*—form; *kalyāṇa-tamam*—auspicious; *tat*—that; *te*—your; *paśyāmi*—I may see; *yaḥ*—one who is; *asau*—the sun; *asau*—that; *puruṣaḥ*—Personality of Godhead; *saḥ*—He; *aham*—myself; *asmi*—I am.

TRANSLATION

O my Lord, O primeval Philosopher, Maintainer of the universe, O regulating Principle, Destination of the pure devotees, Well-wisher of the progenitors of mankind, please remove the effulgence of Your transcendental rays, so that I can see Your Form of Bliss. You are the eternal Supreme Personality of Godhead, like unto the Sun, as am I.

PURPORT

The Sun and the Sun's rays are one and the same qualitatively. Similarly, the Lord and the living entities are one and the same in quality. The Sun is one, but the molecules of the Sun's rays are innumerable. The Sun's rays constitute part of the Sun; the Sun and the rays conjointly are the complete Sun. Within the Sun planet there is the Sun god, and similarly within the supreme spiritual planet, *Goloka Vṛndavan,* from which the effulgent *Brahma-jyoti* is emanating, there is the eternal Lord, as is stated in the *Brahma-saṁhitā:*

> The transcendental Abode of Lord Kṛṣṇa is the land of touchstones, of which the houses are built, shaded by desire trees. The Lord is engaged there in herding the *surabhi*

cows, and is always served and surrounded by thousands of Goddesses of Fortune, who wait upon Him with all respect.

The description of this transcendental Abode of Lord Kṛṣṇa is in the *Brahma-saṁhitā,* and the *Brahma-jyoti* is described there as the supreme rays from that planet, just as the Sun's rays come from the Sun globe. Unless one surpasses the *Brahma-jyoti* glare, one cannot have any information of the land of the Lord. The impersonalist philosopher, being blinded by the dazzling *Brahma-jyoti,* cannot realize the factual Abode of the Lord, nor His transcendental form. Affected by such a poor fund of knowledge, the thinkers cannot understand the all-blissful transcendental form of Lord Kṛṣṇa. *Śrī Īśopaniṣad,* therefore, offers this prayer to the Lord to remove the effulgent rays of the *Brahma-jyoti,* so that the pure devotee can see His all-blissful transcendental form.

By realization of the impersonal *Brahma-jyoti,* one experiences the auspicious aspect of the Supreme; by experience of the *Paramātman,* or all-pervading feature of the Supreme, one experiences a still more auspicious enlightenment, and by meeting the Personality of Godhead face to face, the devotee experiences the most auspicious feature of the Supreme. Being addressed as the Philosopher, the Maintainer, the Well-wisher, and so forth, the Supreme Truth cannot be considered impersonal. That is the indication of *Śrī Īśopaniṣad.* The word Maintainer is especially significant: The Lord maintains His devotees specifically, although He is the Maintainer of one and all beings. By surpassing the impersonal *Brahma-jyoti,* when the devotee sees the personal aspect of the Lord and His most auspicious eternal form, then the devotee realizes the Absolute Truth in full. Srīla Jīva Gosvāmī says in his *Bhāgavata-sandarbha* as follows:

The complete conception of the Absolute Truth is realized in the Personality of Godhead, because He is Almighty, with full potency in transcendence. In the *Brahma-jyoti* the full potency of the Absolute Truth is not realized, and therefore *Brahman* realization is only partial realization of the Personality of Godhead. O learned sages, the first letter of the word *Bhagavān* is twice significant: first in the sense of "one who fully maintains", and second in the sense of "guardian". The second letter—*ga*—means guide, leader or creator. The letter *va* (or *ba)* means that every being lives in Him, and He also lives in every being. In other words, the transcendental sound *Bhagavān* represents the infinite knowledge, potency, energy, opulence, strength and influence, all without any tinge of material inebrieties.

The Lord fully maintains His unalloyed devotees, and He guides such devotees progressively on the path of devotional perfection. As Leader of His devotees, He ultimately awards the desired result of devotional service by giving Himself to His devotees. The devotees of the Lord see the Lord eye to eye by the causeless mercy of the Lord, and thus the Lord helps His devotees to reach the supermost spiritual planet, *Goloka Vṛndavan.* As Creator, He can create all the necessary qualifications in His devotee so that the devotee can ultimately reach Him. The Lord is the Cause of all causes, and there is no cause of Him, for He is the Original Cause. As such He enjoys His own Self by manifesting His own internal potency.

The external potency is manifested not exactly by Himself, for He expands Himself as the *Puruṣas*, and it is in these forms that He maintains the features of the material manifestation. By such expansions does He create, maintain and annihilate the cosmic manifestation.

The living entities are also differentiated expansions of His Self, and because some of the living entities desire to be lord, imitating the Supreme Lord, He allows them to enter into the cosmic creation, with the option of fully utilizing their propensity for lording it over. On account of the presence of His parts and parcels, the living entities, the whole phenomenal world is stirred into action and reaction. The living entities are given full facility to lord it over material Nature, but the ultimate controller is the Lord Himself in His plenary feature of *Paramātman,* the Supersoul, which is one of the *Puruṣas.*

Therefore, there is a gulf of difference between the living entity known as *ātman,* and the controlling Lord, known as *Paramātman*—the soul and the Supersoul. *Paramātman* is the controller, and *ātman* is controlled; therefore they cannot be on the same level. The *Paramātman* fully cooperates with the *ātman,* and thus He is known as the constant companion of the living being.

This all-pervading feature of the Lord, Which exists in all circumstances of waking and sleeping, and also in potential states, and from Which the *jīva-śakti* (living force) is generated—as both the conditioned and the liberated souls—is known as *Brahman.*

Thus the Lord is the Origin of both *Paramātman* and *Brahman,* and therefore He is the Origin of all living entities, and all else that exists. One who knows this engages himself at once in the devotional service of the Lord. Such a pure and fully cognizant devotee of the Lord is fully attached to Him in heart and soul, and whenever such a devotee assembles with similar devotees, they have no other engagement but to glorify the Lord in terms of His transcendental activities. Those who are not as perfect as the pure devotees, those who have realized only the *Brahman* feature or the *Paramātman* feature of the Lord, cannot appreciate the activities of such perfect devotees. But the Lord always helps such pure devotees by supplying necessary knowledge within their hearts, and by His special favor He dissipates all the darkness of ignorance. This the philosophers and *yogis* cannot imagine, because they more or less depend on their own strength. As is stated in the *Kaṭha Upaniṣad,* the Lord can be known only to those whom He favors, and not to anyone else. And such special favors are bestowed upon His pure devotees only. *Śrī Īśopaniṣad* here indicates such favor of the Lord, beyond the purview of the *Brahma-jyoti.*

Mantra Seventeen

वायुरनिलममृतमथेदं भस्मान्तं शरीरम् ।
ॐ क्रतो स्मर कृतं स्मर क्रतो स्मर कृतं स्मर ॥ १७ ॥

vāyur anilam amṛtam
athedaṁ bhasmāntaṁ śarīram
om krato smara kṛtaṁ smara
krato smara kṛtaṁ smara.

vāyuḥ—air of life; *anilam*—total reservoir of air; *amṛtam*—indestructible; *atha*—now; *idam*—this; *bhasmāntam*—after being turned into ashes; *śarīram*—body; *om*—O Lord; *krato*—the Enjoyer of all sacrifices; *smara*—please remember; *kṛtam*—all that has been done by me; *smara*—please remember; *krato*—the Supreme Beneficiary; *smara*—please remember; *kṛtam*—all that I have done for You; *smara*—please remember.

TRANSLATION

Let this temporary body be burnt into ashes, and let the air of life be merged with the totality of air. Now, O my Lord, please remember all my sacrifices, and because You are the ultimate Beneficiary, please remember all that I have done for You.

PURPORT

This temporary material body is certainly a foreign dress. In the *Bhagavad-gītā* it is clearly said that after the destruction of the material body, the living entity is not annihilated, nor does he lose his identity. The identity of the living entity is never, therefore, impersonal or without form; but on the contrary, it is the material dress which is formless, and which takes a shape according to the form of the indestructible person. No living entity is originally formless, as is wrongly supposed by persons with a poor fund of knowledge. Here also in *Mantra* Seventeen of *Śrī Īśopaniṣad,* the principle is supported that the living entity exists after the annihilation of the material body.

In the material world there is wonderful workmanship by material Nature in the matter of creating different varieties of bodies for the living beings, in terms of their propensities for sense gratification. The one who wanted to taste stool is given a material body which is quite suitable for eating stool—that of a hog. Similarly, the tiger has such a body that it can live by enjoying the blood of other animals, and by eating their flesh.

The human being is not meant for eating stool or flesh, because the shape of the teeth is different. Nor does he have any desire to taste stool, even in the most aboriginal state of life. Human teeth are so made that they can chew and cut fruit and vegetables, with two canine teeth so that one can eat flesh also. The material bodies of all animals and men are foreign to the living entity, and change according to the desire of the being for sense gratification. In this cycle of evolution one changes bodies one after another: from aquatic life—when the world was full of water—to vegetable life, from vegetable life to worm life, from worm life to bird life, from bird life to animal life, and from animal life to the human form.

The highest development of life is this human form when it is possessed of a full sense of spiritual knowledge, and the highest development of spiritual sense is described in this *mantra* of the *Veda:* one should give up this material body to be turned into ashes, and allow the living air to merge into the eternal reservoir of air. The living being's activities are performed within the body by movements of different kinds of air, and this is called, in sum, the *prāṇa-vāyu.* The *yogis* generally study to control the airs of the body, and the soul is supposed to rise up from one circle of air to another till it rises onto the *brahma-randhra,* or highest circle of air. Then the perfect *yogi* can transfer himself to any planet he likes. The process is to give up one material body and then enter into another body, and the highest perfection of such a bodily change is possible when the living entity is able to give up this material body altogether, as is suggested in this *mantra.* He may then enter into the spiritual atmosphere, where he develops a completely different quality of body—a spiritual body—which never has to meet death or change.

Here in the material world one has to change his body, forced by material Nature on account of his different desires for sense gratification. These desires are represented in the various species of life, from the germs to the most perfect material bodies, those of Brahmā and the demigods. All of these have bodies of matter in different shapes, and the intelligent person sees oneness not in the variety of bodies, but in the spiritual identity.

The spiritual spark which is the part and parcel of the Supreme Lord is the same either in the body of a hog or in the body of a demigod. There are different bodies according to the pious and vicious activities of the living entity. The human body is highly developed, with full consciousness of the constitution of the body; and the most perfect man, according to the Vedic scriptures, surrenders unto the Lord after many, many births of culturing knowledge. The culture of knowledge reaches perfection only when the knower comes to the point of surrendering unto the Supreme Lord, called Vāsudeva. But even after attaining knowledge in the matter of one's spiritual identity, unless he comes to the point of knowing that the living entities are eternal parts and parcels of the Whole, and that they can never become the Whole, one has to fall down again into the material atmosphere, even after having become one with the *Brahma-jyoti.*

The *Brahma-jyoti* emanating from the transcendental body of the Lord is full of spiritual sparks. The spiritual sparks being individual identities with the full sense of existence, sometimes desire to become the enjoyers of the senses, and thus they are given places in the material world to become false lords, under the dictation of the senses. This sense of overlordship is the material disease of the living being, and under the spell of such sense enjoyment he transmigrates through the different shapes of body manifested in the material world. The sense of becoming one with the *Brahma-jyoti* is not, therefore, mature knowledge. The sense of surrendering unto the Lord completely, and developing the sense of spiritual service is the highest perfectional stage.

In this *mantra* the living entity prays to enter into the spiritual Kingdom of God after relinquishing the material body and the material air. The devotee prays to the Lord to remember his activities and the sacrifices he has performed, now before his material body is turned into ashes. This prayer is made at the time of death, with full consciousness of his past deeds and of the ultimate goal. One who is completely under the rules of material law remembers the heinous activities performed during the existence of his material body, and therefore he gets another material body after death. The *Bhagavad-gītā* confirms this truth. It states that at the time of death, the mind carries with it the propensities of the dying animal, and the next life is obtained in terms of that mental state.

Unlike the simple animals, who have no developed mind, the human being can remember the activities of his passing life like dreams at night, and therefore his mind remains surcharged with material desires, and he cannot enter into the spiritual kingdom with a spiritual body. The devotees, however, by practice of devotional service to the Lord, develop a sense of love for Godhead. And even if at the time of death a devotee does not remember his godly service, the Lord does not forget him. This prayer is to remind the Lord about the devotee's sacrifices, but even if there is no reminder, the Lord does not forget the devotional service of the pure devotee.

The Lord clearly describes His intimate relationship with His devotees in the *Gītā*. Śrīla Bhaktivinode Thākur explains the *Gītā's* verses in this connection:

> One should accept a devotee who is on the right path of the saints, even though such a devotee may seem of loose character. One should try to understand the real import of the words "loose character". A conditioned soul has to act in double functions,

namely one for the maintenance of the body, and again for self realization. Social status, mental development, cleanliness, austerity, nourishment and the struggle for existence, are all for the maintenance of the body. And the self realization part of his activities is executed in his occupation as a devotee of the Lord, and he performs action in that connection also. These two different functions go along parallel lines because a conditioned soul cannot give up the maintenance of the body. The proportion of activities for maintenance of the body decreases, however, in proportion to the increase in devotional service. And as long as the proportion of devotional service does not come to the right point, there is a chance for an occasional exhibition of worldliness. But it should be noted that such worldliness cannot continue for any length of time because, by the grace of the Lord, such imperfections will come to an end very shortly. Therefore, the path of devotional service is the only right path. Being on the right path, even an occasional occurrence of worldliness does not hamper one in the advancement of self realization.

And, in the *Gītā* Itself, Kṛṣṇa says:

One who is engaged in devotional service, despite the most abominable action, is to be considered saintly because he is rightly situated. Very shortly does he become righteous, and attain to lasting peace. O son of Kuntī, it is My promise that My devotee will never perish. O son of Pṛthā, anyone who will take shelter in Me, whether a woman or a merchant or born in a low family, can yet approach the Supreme Destination. How much greater then are the *Brāhmaṇas,* the righteous, the devotees and saintly kings! In this miserable world, these are fixed in devotional service to the Lord. Engage in My service, and surrender unto Me. Completely absorbed in Me, surely will you come to Me. (*Gītā*, IX/30-34)

Such facilities of devotional service are denied the impersonalists because they are attached to the *Brahma-jyoti* feature of the Lord. They can neither penetrate the *Brahma-jyoti,* as is suggested in the previous *mantras,* nor do they believe in the Personality of Godhead. Their business is mostly concerned with semantics, the jugglery of words of mental creation. As such the impersonalists pursue fruitless labor, as is confirmed in the *Bhagavad-gītā* in the Twelfth Chapter.

All the facilities suggested in this *mantra* of *Śrī Iśopaniṣad* can easily be obtained by constant contact with the Personal feature of the Absolute Truth. Devotional service to the Lord consists essentially of nine transcendental activities on the part of the devotee:

1. hearing about the Lord,
2. glorifying the Lord,
3. remembering the Lord,
4. serving the Lotus Feet of the Lord,
5. worshiping the Lord,
6. offering prayers to the Lord,
7. serving the Lord,
8. friendly association with the Lord,
9. surrendering everything unto the Lord.

These nine principles of devotional service, either in sum total or one by one, can help the devotee to be constantly in touch with God, and therefore at the end of life it is easy for the devotee to remember the Lord. By adopting only one of these nine principles it was possible for the following renowned devotees of the Lord to achieve the highest perfection:

1. By hearing only, Mahārāj Parīkṣit, the hero of *Śrīmad-Bhāgavatam,* achieved the desired result.

2. Just by glorifying the Lord, Śukadeva Gosvāmī, the speaker of *Srimad-Bhāgavatam,* achieved his perfection.
3. By praying, Akrūra achieved the desired result.
4. By remembering, Prahlāda Mahārāj achieved the desired result.
5. By worshiping, Pṛthu Mahārāj achieved perfection.
6. By serving the Lotus Feet of the Lord, the Goddess of Fortune, Lakṣmī, achieved perfection.
7. By personal service to the Lord, Hanuman achieved the desired result.
8. By friendship, Arjuna achieved the result.
9. By surrendering everything that he had, Mahārāj Bali achieved the desired result.

Actually, the explanation of this *mantra* and of practically all the *mantras* of the Vedic hymns is summarized in the *Vedānta-sūtras;* and then again they are properly explained in the *Śrīmad-Bhāgavatam. Śrīmad-Bhāgavatam* is the mature fruit of the Vedic tree of wisdom. In the *Śrīmad-Bhāgavatam* this particular *mantra* is explained in the questions and answers of Mahārāj Parīkṣit and Gosvāmī Śukadeva at the very beginning of their meeting. As hearing and chanting of the science of God is the basic principle of devotional life, so the complete *Bhāgavatam* is heard by Mahārāj Parīkṣit and chanted by Gosvāmī Śukadeva. Mahārāj Parīkṣit enquired from Śukadeva because Śukadeva was a greater spiritual master than any great *yogi* or transcendentalist of his time.

Mahārāj Parīkṣit's question was, "What is the duty of every man, specifically at the time of death?"

The answer by Gosvāmī Śukadeva was that everyone who is desirous of being free from all anxieties should always hear about and glorify the Personality of Godhead, Who is the Supreme Director of everything, the Extinguisher of all difficulties, and the Supersoul of all living entities.

So-called human society is generally engaged at night in the matter of sleeping or sex indulgence. And during the daytime men are engaged in earning money as much as possible, or else in shopping for the family maintenance. People have very little time to talk about the Personality of Godhead or to make any enquiries about Him. They have dismissed the case of God's existence in so many ways, especially by declaring Him to be impersonal—that is, without any sense perception. But in the Vedic literature, whether the *Upaniṣads* or the *Vedānta-sūtras* or the *Bhagavad-gītā* or the *Śrīmad-Bhāgavatam,* in every scripture it is declared that the Lord is the sentient Being, supreme over all other living entities. And His glorious activities are identical with Himself. One should therefore not indulge in hearing and speaking of the rubbish activities of worldly politicians and the so-called big men of society, but should so mold his life that not a second is wasted without engagement in godly activities.

Śrī Īśopaniṣad directs us towards such activities.

Unless one is accustomed to this devotional practice, what will he remember at the time of death when the body is dislocated, and how can he pray to the Almighty Lord to remember his sacrifices? Sacrifice means sacrificing the interest of the senses. One has to learn this art by employing the senses in the service of the Lord during one's lifetime, so that one can utilize the result at the time of death.

Mantra Eighteen

अग्ने नय सुपथा राये अस्मान् विश्वानि देव वयुनानि विद्वान् ।
युयोध्यस्मज्जुहुराणमेनो भूयिष्ठां ते नमउक्तिं विधेम ॥१८॥

agne naya supathārāye asmān
viśvāni deva vayunāni vidvān
yuyodhy asmaj juhurāṇam eno
bhūyiṣṭhāṁ te nama-uktiṁ vidhema.

agne—O my Lord, powerful like the fire; *naya*—kindly lead me; *supathā*—in the right path; *rāye*—O the Omnipotent; *asmān*—all of us; *viśvāni*—everything including; *deva*—O my Lord; *vayunāni*—all actions; *vidvān*—the knower; *yuyodhi*—get me freed from; *asmat*—ourselves; *juhurāṇam*—all hindrances on the path; *enas*—all vices; *bhūyiṣṭhām*—being fallen on the ground; *te*—unto you; *namāḥ*—of obeisances; *uktim*—words; *vidhema*— do I act.

TRANSLATION

O my Lord, powerful as the fire, Omnipotent One, now I do offer You all obeisances, falling at Your Feet on the ground. O my Lord, please lead me on the right path to reach You, and, as You know all of what I have done in the past, please make me free from the reactions to my past sins, so that there will be no hindrance to my progress.

PURPORT

This surrendering process and praying for the causeless mercy of the Lord leads the devotee progressively on the path of complete self realization. The Lord is addressed as the fire because He can burn anything into ashes—including the sins of the surrendered soul. As described in the previous *mantras,* the real or ultimate aspect of the Absolute is His feature as the Personality of Godhead. His impersonal feature of the *Brahma-jyoti* is a dazzling covering over the face of the Lord. Fruitive activities, or the *karma-kāṇḍa* path of self realization, is the lowest stage in this endeavor. As soon as such activities become even slightly deviated from the regulative principles of the *Vedas,* such activities are transformed into *vikarma,* or acts against the interest of the actor. Such *vikarma* is enacted by the illusioned living entities simply for sense gratification, and thus such activities become hindrances on the path of self realization.

Self realization is possible for the human form of life, but not for other forms. There are 8,400,000 species or forms of life—of which the human form, with the qualifications of Brahminical culture, presents the only chance to obtain knowledge of the Transcendence. Brahminical culture means truthfulness, controlling the senses, forbearance, simplicity, full knowledge, full faith in God—and not to become simply proud of one's high parentage. To be the son of a *Brāhmaṇa* is a chance to become a *Brāhmaṇa*, just as being the son of a big man is a chance to become a big man. But such a birthright is not everything, because one still has to attain the Brahminical qualifications for himself. As soon as one becomes proud of his birth as the son of a *Brāhmaṇa* and neglects to acquire the qualifications of a real *Brāhmaṇa,* he at once becomes degraded and drawn from the path of self realization, and his life-mission as a human being is defeated.

In the *Bhagavad-gītā* it is assured us by the Lord that the *yoga-bhraṣṭas,* or souls fallen from the path of self realization, are given a chance for rectification by taking birth either in the families of good *Brāhmaṇas* or in the families of rich merchants. These are the higher chances for self realization: to become a rich man's son, or to become the son of a good *Brāhmaṇa.* And if these chances are misused by the illusioned human being, the result is that such a man loses the good chance of human life offered by the Almighty Lord.

The regulative principles are such that one who follows them is promoted from the plane of fruitive activities to the plane of transcendental knowledge, and from transcendental knowledge he becomes perfect, after many, many births, when he surrenders unto the Lord. This is the general procedure. But one who surrenders at the very beginning, as is mentioned in this *mantra,* at once surpasses all the stages of progression by simple adoption of the devotional attitude. As is stated in the *Gītā,* the Lord at once takes charge of such a surrendered soul and makes him free from all the reactions to his sinful acts. In the *karma-kāṇḍa* activities there are many sinful actions, and in *jñāna-kāṇḍa,* the path of philosophical development, the number of such actions is less. But in devotional service to the Lord, the path of *bhakti,* there is practically no chance of sinful reactions. One who is a devotee of the Lord attains all the good qualifications of the Lord Himself, not to mention becoming a *Brāhmaṇa.* A devotee automatically attains the qualifications of an expert *Brāhmaṇa* authorized to perform sacrifices, even though such a devotee may not have taken his birth in the family of a *Brāhmaṇa.* Such is the omnipotence of the Lord that He can make a man born in the family of a *Brāhmaṇa* as degraded as a lowborn dog-eater, and He can also make a lowborn dog-eater more than a qualified *Brāhmaṇa,* simply on the strength of devotional service.

The omnipotent Lord, being situated within the heart of everyone, can give directions to His sincere devotee as to the right path. Such directions are especially offered to the devotee, even if he desires something else. For others God gives sanction to the doer only at the risk of the doer, but in the case of a devotee the Lord directs him in such a way that he never acts wrongly. In the *Śrīmad-Bhāgavatam* it is said that the Lord is so kind upon His devotee that even though he sometimes falls into the entanglement of *vikarma*—acts against the directions of the *Vedas*—the Lord at once rectifies the mistakes of the devotee from within his heart, because such devotees are very dear to the Lord.

Here in this *mantra* the devotee prays to the Lord to rectify him from within his heart. To err is human: A conditioned soul is very often apt to commit mistakes, and the only remedial measure for such unknown sins is to give oneself up to the Lotus Feet of the Lord, so that He may guide the devotee. The Lord takes this charge for the fully surrendered souls, and thus all problems are solved simply by surrendering oneself unto the Lord and acting in terms of the Lord's directions. Such directions are given to the sincere devotee in two ways. One is by means of the saints, scriptures, and spiritual master; and the other is by the Lord Himself, residing within the heart of everyone. Thus the devotee is protected in all respects.

The Vedic knowledge is transcendental and it cannot be understood simply by mundane educational procedures. One can understand the Vedic *mantras* only by the grace of the

Lord and the spiritual master. If one takes shelter of a bona fide spiritual master, it is to be understood that he has obtained the grace of the Lord. The Lord appears as the spiritual master for the devotee. And so the spiritual master, the Vedic injunctions, and the Lord Himself from within all guide the devotee in full strength, and there is no chance of such a devotee falling again into the mire of material illusion. The devotee, thus protected all around, is sure to reach the ultimate destination of perfection. The whole process is hinted at in this *mantra* of *Śrī Īśopaniṣad,* and the *Śrīmad-Bhāgavatam* still further explains this.

Hearing and chanting of the glories of the Lord are themselves acts of piety. The Lord wants everyone to do this, because He is the Well-wisher of all living entities. And by practicing this hearing and chanting of the glories of the Lord, one becomes cleansed of all undesirable things within himself. His devotion becomes fixed upon the Lord. At this stage the devotee acquires the Brahminical qualifications, and the resultant reactions of lower qualities become completely vanished. He becomes fully enlightened by such devotional service and thus knows the path of the Lord and how to attain Him. All doubts become diminished, and he becomes a pure devotee.

Thus end the Bhaktivedānta Purports to Śrī Īśopaniṣad, the knowledge that brings one nearer to the Supreme Personality of Godhead, Kṛṣṇa.

APPENDIX 1

ABOUT THE AUTHOR

His Divine Grace A.C. Bhaktivedānta Swāmī Prabhupāda was born Abhay Charan De on September 1, 1896 in Calcutta. In 1920 he finished his schooling, majoring in philosophy, English and economics at the University of Calcutta. Soon afterward, Abhay Charan De took up the duties of manager of a large chemical concern. Then in 1922, he met His Divine Grace Śrī Śrīmad Bhakti Siddhānta Sarasvatī Gosvāmī Mahārāj, the founder of 64 Gauḍīya Vaiṣṇava Maṭhs in India, Berlin and London. Bhaktivedānta Swāmī recently recalled the key to his approaching his spiritual master: "When I first started going to see my Guru Mahārāj, he said of me, 'This boy hears very nicely. He does not go away. So I shall make him a disciple.' That was my qualification, or whatever you may call it. I would simply ask when Guru Mahārāj would speak, then I'd sit down and go on hearing. I would understand, or not understand; others would disperse, I'd not disperse. So he remarked, 'This boy is interested to hear'. Because I was serious in hearing, therefore I am now serious about *kīrtanam*, which means speaking or preaching. If one has heard nicely, then he will speak nicely."

At Allahabad in 1933, Abhay Charan De was formally initiated, and in 1936, just days before Bhakti Siddhānta Sarasvatī's departure from this mortal world, he was specifically ordered to spread Kṛṣṇa Consciousness in the English language to the West.

A.C. Bhaktivedānta Swāmī, known as Prabhupāda to his disciples, has told us that at first he did not take the mission given to him by his spiritual master with the utmost seriousness. But then he was reading a *Bhagavad-gītā* commentary written by Śrīla Bhaktivinode Thākur, who was the father of Bhakti Siddhānta Sarasvatī and the pioneer of the Kṛṣṇa Consciousness movement in the modern age. Śrīla Bhaktivinode has written that just as one cannot separate the body from the soul while in this conditioned state, so the disciple cannot separate the spiritual master's order from his very life. Bhaktivedānta Swāmī took these words seriously, and gradually his whole life became dedicated to carrying out the orders of his Guru Mahārāj. In 1959 he took *sannyāsa*, the renounced order of spiritual life, and in 1965, at the advanced age of 70, A.C. Bhaktivedānta Swāmī arrived in New York City to fulfill his master's sacred mission.

One must try to understand that Śrīla Prabhupāda is neither an Indian author nor Indian culturist nor Hindu sectarian. The first teaching of the *Bhagavad-gītā* is that no one is Indian, no one is American—our real self is beyond this temporary bodily designation; our permanent identity, eternal, blissful and full of knowledge, is with the Supreme Personality of Godhead as His eternal servant; and our position is to be situated beyond the material universes in the spiritual planets, within the spiritual sky. This is the platform of Kṛṣṇa Consciousness.

To think, "I am American," "I am Russian," etc. is our disease, and is due to forgetfulness of our eternal nature as spirit soul. Unfortunately, under the spell of illusion, every embodied creature is satisfied with his present material body. Even the worm in the stool is thinking, "I am all right." Despite so many disadvantages and miseries, all living entities are engaged in satisfying their senses and are thinking it is all right. Therefore when the bona fide *guru* comes with the transcendental message, calling the souls back to home, back to Godhead, they do not want to come out of material encagement. Often, people prefer to be encouraged in illusion and therefore pay fees to learn that they are God or equal to God in all respects and thus "free" to go on "enjoying" material life of sense gratification. So we see *yoga* and meditation teachers advertising that they will improve one's material facilities. They overlook the fact that elimination of sense gratification is the first step in the standard *yoga* or transcendental system. A.C. Bhaktivedānta Swāmī does not encourage unrestricted sense gratification, or the belief that one is God, or that God is impersonal or void. He is passing on, *as it is,* the information from Vedic literature, that the Supreme Personality of Godhead is a Person and that devotional service unto Him is the perfection of all purificatory processes. Lord Kṛṣṇa in *Bhagavad-gītā* is recognized as the Supreme Lord, and *Srī Īśopaniṣad* confirms the Personality of Godhead as the anti-material Supreme Controller and the only Enjoyer. A.C. Bhaktivedānta Swāmī is teaching surrender to Kṛṣṇa, the Supreme Lord.

Śrīla Prabhupāda is the living example of the saintly person pointed to in all Vedic literature who is personally free from all material contamination and active in spiritual understanding. He is the Kṛṣṇa conscious personality who is so dear to Kṛṣṇa, who understands that the highest welfare is not to pose oneself as the friend of humanity, but to teach that God or Kṛṣṇa is the dear-most Friend Who alone is capable of alleviating the misery of each and every living entity. A.C. Bhaktivedānta is teaching what is really common sense to our intelligence, but we are so bewildered by the glitter of the material nature that we are distracted from his message. He is simply canvassing for God on the order of his spiritual master. Once Śrīla Prabhupāda was asked, "Are you an incarnation of God?" "No," he answered, "I am servant of God." Then he paused and went on, "Not exactly servant. To be servant of God is not an ordinary thing." The servants or devotees of Kṛṣṇa are so great that they are beyond the desire to merge with God. Sometimes, in their intimate association and exchange with God, they even become "greater" than Him, as when He allows some devotee to become His mother or lover. Prabhupāda's mission is not less than to distribute this topmost love of God to all persons. It is stated in the Vedic literature that a small man wants to make only himself happy, a somewhat bigger man wants to make his family or his country happy, but the great man wants to make all persons happy.

Bhaktivedānta Swāmī produces his books by speaking them on a dictaphone. He is presently working on five books at once. These books are a matter of realization. As he has said, "When you become self-realized you automatically write volumes of books." And one of the qualifications of a devotee is that he is poetic. Śrīla Prabhupāda is always immersed in

Kṛṣṇa by speaking, dictating, singing about Kṛṣṇa's Glories, preaching formally at meetings or planning the expansion of the Kṛṣṇa Consciousness movement. In the *Bhagavad-gītā*, Seventh Chapter, it is stated that out of thousands of men few seek perfection, and out of the thousands who attain perfection hardly one knows Kṛṣṇa. Lord Kṛṣṇa also declares in the Eighteenth Chapter that the dearmost devotee of all is he who spreads the teaching of love of Kṛṣṇa: "Never will there be one dearer to Me." Bhaktivedānta Swāmī's spiritual master, Bhakti Siddhānta Sarasvatī, once drew a picture of a *mṛdanga* (drum used on *Saṅkīrtan*) and, beside it, a printing press. He said that the *mṛdanga* can be heard for several blocks, but that the press can be heard around the world. He therefore called the printing press "the big *mṛdanga*". For the purpose of worldwide service to humanity, ISKCON Press has been established, for the exclusive printing of Śrīla Prabhupāda's books.

In 1968, Macmillan published *The Bhagavad Gītā As It Is* translated with commentary by A.C. Bhaktivedānta Swāmī. The *Gītā* is the gist of the entire Vedic literature. Just this one book can free anyone from the clutches of material nature and fix one in eternal loving service unto Śri Kṛṣṇa the Personality of Godhead. As originally written by Śrīla Prabhupāda, the manuscript of *The Bhagavad Gītā As It Is* is many times larger than the version published by Macmillan. Publication of this original, expanded version is being undertaken by ISKCON. Another important published literature by Prabhupāda is his *Teachings of Lord Chaitanya*. This book outlines the precepts of Caitanya Mahāprabhu, the Golden Avatar Who appeared in India 500 years ago and propagated the Hare Kṛṣṇa *mantra* as the means of God realization for the present age. A book called *Nectar of Devotion*, an authorized summary study of Śrī Rūpa

Gosvāmī's *Bhakti-rasāmṛta-sindhu,* will also soon be published. Prabhupāda is presently writing a several volume work called Kṛṣṇa, which contains all of the Pastimes of the Supreme Lord when present on this planet 5000 years ago. Translations are also underway of the *Vedānta-sūtras, Caitanya-caritāmṛta* and his 12 volumes of *Śrīmad-Bhāgavatam.* The literatures compiled by A.C. Bhaktivedānta Swāmī are authorized by the disciplic succession, which is descending from Kṛṣṇa Himself; Prabhupāda's whole life mission is to faithfully pass on the original understanding of Kṛṣṇa Consciousness without distortion. According to the Vedic literature this descending process is the only way to realization of the Absolute Truth, as the Absolute Truth is beyond the reach of our mundane speculation or scholarship.

The author is not a retired personality, despite his prodigious literary output. He personally and very intimately guides his disciples through the most practical problems of daily life. Spiritual life is practical and, due to the predominent material atmosphere of *Kali-yuga,* often problematic. As spiritual master, Bhaktivedānta Swāmī is the last recourse and the ultimate standard of Kṛṣṇa Consciousness, and he writes some 25 letters a day to leaders and students of his various world-wide centers. He himself resides in no one place but travels from center to center and regularly lectures. The spiritual master is responsible for his devotees; when he accepts a sincere soul as his disciple, he promises to take him back to home, back to Godhead. No one should think, "Oh, everyone is taking a spiritual master; let me take one." The spiritual master as a style or as a pet is useless. Rather, his order is to be taken as one's life and soul. By taking shelter at the feet of the bona fide guru and serving him 24 hours a day, the fallen soul can be lifted to the spiritual sky. It is said that if the spiritual master is pleased, then one can make great advances in spiritual life. And one pure convinced devotee can make many pure devotees by his example and teachings. Those serious students with an understanding of the absolute value of the spiritual platform of life therefore honor the spiritual master with the honor due to God, because the *guru* is the transparent via media or representative of God and is distributing unalloyed love of God. The intelligent reader is invited to take to this philosophy with the utmost seriousness.

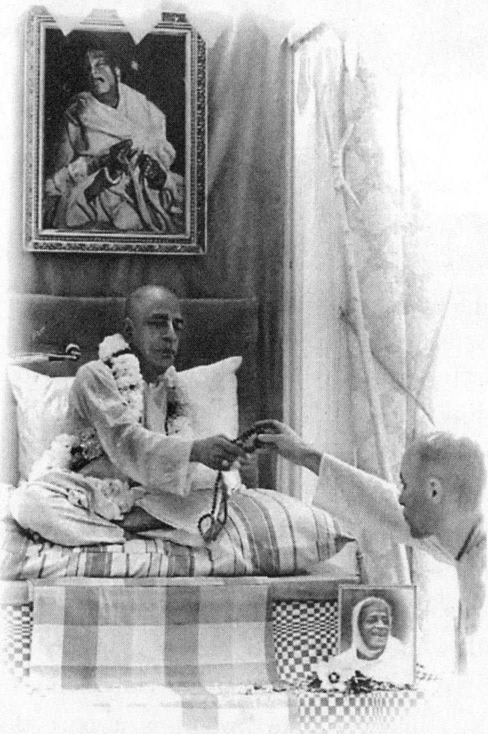

APPENDIX 2

What Is The International Society For Krishna Consciousness?

The International Society for Kṛṣṇa Consciousness was formed in July, 1966 by His Divine Grace A.C. Bhaktivedānta Swāmī Prabhupāda and a number of his American students. ISKCON is composed of devotees. Devotees are held together by mutual agreement to accept the principles of Bhakti-yoga or devotional service as the goal of life. By mutual endeavor, the entire Society concentrates on Śrī Kṛṣṇa, the Personality of Godhead, while engaged in various tasks, cooking, eating, working in an office or chanting the Holy Names in the city streets. A.C. Bhaktivedānta Swāmī is a pure devotee, and those disciples who sincerely follow his instructions have every chance of becoming pure devotees themselves. The initiated devotees in each center live in urban commune settings (with the one exception of New Vrindaban, ISKCON's *ashram* of homes, temples, farm land and cows in the hills of West Virginia), and are freeing themselves from the conditions of birth, death, disease and old age by fixing their minds on the eternal joyful Personality of Godhead. To live in ISKCON as an initiated student, one agrees to accept four rules: no meat-eating, no illicit sex, no intoxicants and no gambling. The disciples perform devotional service, duties and chanting in a life-routine characterized by simple living and high thinking.

Kṛṣṇa Consciousness is experienced as a process of self-purification. Its means and ends are an open secret, and there is no financial charge for learning Kṛṣṇa Consciousness or receiving initiation into the chanting of Hare Kṛṣṇa. The gist of devotional service to Kṛṣṇa is that one takes whatever capacity or talent he or she has and dovetails it with the transcendental interest of the Supreme Enjoyer, the Absolute Truth. The writer or poet writes articles and poems for Kṛṣṇa, and the Society publishes periodicals. The businessman does business in order to sell literature and establish many temples around the world. The householders raise children in the science of God, and husband and wife live in mutual cooperation for spiritual progress. And everyone in ISKCON goes on *Saṅkīrtan*! *Saṅkīrtan* means chanting the *Hare Kṛṣṇa mantra* in the city streets for the benefit of all citizens. A.C. Bhaktivedānta Swāmī has said that the *Saṅkīrtan* party is the heart and soul of the Hare Kṛṣṇa movement. Therefore, in each of the 25 ISKCON centers, *Saṅkīrtan* is carried on several times daily, and all other activity is subsidiary. Our spiritual master stresses this, for we are in the line of Lord Caitanya. Caitanya Mahāprabhu is revealed by Vedic scriptures to be Kṛṣṇa Himself, come in the mood of a pure devotee. Five thousand years ago Lord Caitanya understood from scripture that in this present age of *Kali* (quarrel and disturbance), when mental distraction is high and almost no one is serious about spiritual perfection, chanting alone is the most effective means of God realization. Following the *Saṅkīrtan* process chalked out by Lord Caitanya, the Hare Kṛṣṇa movement of today takes parties of from five to 30 devotees, men wearing saffron robes and women wearing colorful saris. And they celebrate the Holy Name with dancing and melodious chanting.

The *Saṅkīrtan* singing is accompanied with *mṛdanga* drum and pairs of *kartals* (hand cymbals). The devotees experience that this joyous singing of the Names of God produces immediate feelings of ecstasy coming from the spiritual stratum. The effect is a clearing away of the dirt from the mind engrossed in the gloom of material existence. Under the instruction of the spiritual master, they gladly spread this chanting, and in reciprocation Śrī Kṛṣṇa allows all to taste the nectar for which everyone is always anxious. Because the Personality of Godhead is Absolute, His Name is nondifferent from Himself. Therefore the Supreme Person, Kṛṣṇa, the Reservoir of Pleasure, dances on the tongue of the chanter of His Name; to chant and hear fixes the mind, in meditation, in direct contact with God. The mantra is not to be mistaken for an ordinary song or anything tinged with the mundane; it is a pure transcendental sound vibration of the Absolute and has been upheld as such since time immemorial by the great sages and Vedic scriptures. Lord Caitanya prays to the Supreme: "My dear Lord, You are so kind that You have invested all potency in Your Holy Name." This Absolute Presence of God in His Name holds true not only for the members of the *Saṅkīrtan* party, but for any living entity who hears the chanting; anyone will benefit if he simply likes the sound of the chanting, or if he appreciates the presence of the *Saṅkīrtan* party in any way. That is the Mercy of the Absolute. The Holy Name is compared to a fire; whether one is scientifically conversant with all the properties of fire or knows nothing about it, if one puts his hand in fire he will be burnt. Sincere chanting and hearing of the *Mahāmantra* will cleanse the mind and elevate one and all to the natural original position of spirit soul. Therefore there is no hesitancy on the devotees' part in going to the largest and most public gatherings of people and broadcasting, wherever possible, the sound of the transcendental Names: Hare Kṛṣṇa, Hare Kṛṣṇa, Kṛṣṇa Kṛṣṇa, Hare Hare / Hare Rāma, Hare Rāma, Rāma Rāma, Hare Hare.

Chanting takes place regularly in the main streets of cities like New York, Los Angeles, Boston, San Francisco, Berkeley, Detroit, Philadelphia, Washington D.C., Honolulu, London, Hamburg, Tokyo, etc., with new ISKCON centers being regularly established. The expansion of Kṛṣṇa Consciousness is realization of the prediction made by Lord Caitanya: "The chanting of Hare Kṛṣna will be heard in every town and village of the world."

The Society is as famous for its Sunday feasts and festivals as for its chanting in the streets. Every Sunday, in each of the ISKCON centers, a grand feast of from 10 to 15 courses of Indian vegetarian food is prepared and distributed for guests. The feasts are arranged around festival days celebrating the Pastimes of Śrī Kṛṣṇa during His Appearance on the earth 5,000 years ago. Plays, puppet shows and chanting are regular items which invite guests to participate in the transcendental glorification of the Personality of Godhead. Kṛṣṇa Consciousness is not a dry philosophy. Residents of San Francisco appreciate the yearly *Ratha-yatra* Festival in which the large cart bearing the Jagannāth Deity is wheeled to the sea. During the Ratha-yatra celebration of 1969, more than 15,000 people followed the regal 8,000 pound cart, and thousands were fed full plates of *prasādam* at the seaside.

The important aim of the festivals, chanting and philosophizing is to engage people in the service of the Personality of Godhead and in feeling His soothing contact. All miseries are caused by forgetfulness of God, and ISKCON, by reviving the lost memory of the Supreme Lord in the minds of the people, is—according to *Bhagavad-gītā*—performing the greatest service and highest welfare work for suffering humanity. Moreover, it is performed in this sublime and easy way, by feasting, dancing, singing and philosophizing.

Sometimes in Lord Caitanya's time, the devotees were accused by the impersonalists of being mere sentimentalists because they were always singing and dancing. The actual fact is that Kṛṣṇa Consciousness is backed by a vast learned literature, the Vedic scriptures such as *Bhagavad-gītā, Śrīmad-Bhāgavatam, Vedānta-sūtra,* the *Upaniṣads, Mahābhārata, Rāmāyaṇa,* etc., so that one could read 24 hours a day without exhausting the Source. All of this Kṛṣṇa Consciousness information is understood by revelation. Simply by applying one's energy in a devotional service attitude, the knowledge becomes known to the devotee through the heart. Classes in the transcendental science of God consciousness or *bhakti-yoga* are held every morning and three nights a week at all ISKCON centers, and the public is freely invited to attend. The *Brahma Sampradāya* disciplic succession, in which A.C. Bhaktivedānta is coming, is particularly noted for being a learned line. There is plenty of philosophy and logic in stock. There are many different religious philosophies and transcendental teachings, but the Kṛṣṇa conscious students and ministers are unique in that they are convinced of the Personality of Godhead. Not just that they have heard "God is great," but they have heard from the spiritual master and continuously hearing from the scriptures just how great He is, how His energies are working and exactly how He is enjoying. There is no literature of theism as voluminous, exacting, consistent and clear as this Vedic literature of Kṛṣṇa Consciousness. The conviction in service of the Supreme Personality of Godhead is due to direct reciprocation with Him. Simply by chanting or hearing the Pastimes of the Personality of Godhead, one is contacting the Absolute—and he can feel it. By engaging the senses, the will, words and energy, the devotees are receiving constant information from the Spiritual World. Kṛṣṇa Himself describes such devotees as the topmost yogis and mystics, so it is no wonder that they are conversant with the nature of God and the way back to Godhead.

ISKCON provides formal education in the highest science, or what *Bhagavad-gītā* calls the "King of Knowledge." According to Vedic sources, education can only be valid when there is spiritual knowledge or self-realization, and a man is said to have no qualifications if he does not know who he is in terms of self-realization or God realization. Learning the texts requires living in accordance with the scriptural injunctions without the slightest deviation. The need for Kṛṣṇa conscious preachers is very great, and it is a full time vocation. The curriculum advances basically from student to minister; after studying and working in a temple for one year, the student may be awarded the title of *bhakti-śāstri,* or ordained minister, with further responsibilities and with advancement of service. He may finally take the renounced order, called *sannyāsa,* and receive the title *svāmī.*

As the philosophy of Kṛṣṇa Consciousness is non-sectarian, any man—Hindu or Christian—will advance in his faith by chanting the Holy Name of God and hearing the *Bhagavad-gītā.* Without knowledge, realization and loving service to the One Supreme God, there can be no religion. Let the inhabitants of this planet rejoice in the *Saṅkīrtan* movement and live to see the fulfillment of the chanting of Hare Kṛṣṇa carried to every town and village. Only in this way can real peace prevail in the world and mankind qualify to enter into the Kingdom of God.

Sanskrit Diacritical Equivalents

(as used in this book)

Vowels

अ a आ ā इ i ई ī उ u ऊ ū ऋ ṛ ॠ ṝ

ऌ ḷ ए e ऐ ai ओ o औ au

ं ṁ (anusvāra) ः ḥ (visarga)

Consonants

Gutturals:	क ka	ख kha	ग ga	घ gha	ङ ṅa
Palatals:	च ca	छ cha	ज ja	झ jha	ञ ña
Cerebrals:	ट ṭa	ठ ṭha	ड ḍa	ढ ḍha	ण ṇa
Dentals:	त ta	थ tha	द da	ध dha	न na
Labials:	प pa	फ pha	ब ba	भ bha	म ma
Semivowels	य ya	र ra	ल la	व va	
Sibilants:	श śa	ष ṣa	स sa		
Aspirate:	ह ha	ऽ = ' (avagraha) – the aphostrophe			

The vowels above should be prononced as follows:

a — like the *a* in org*a*n or the *u* in b*u*t.

ā — like the *ā* in f*a*r but held twice as long as *a*.

i — like the *i* in p*i*n.

ī — like the *ī* in p*i*que but held twice as long as *i*.

u —like the *u* in p*u*sh.

ū — like the ū in r*u*le but held twice as long as *u*.

ṛ — like the *ri* in *Ri*ta (but more like French *ru*).

ṝ — same as ṛi but held twice as long.

lṛ — like lree (lruu).

e — like the *e* in th*e*y.

ai — like the *ai* in *ai*sle.

o — like the *o* in g*o*.

au— like the *ow* in h*ow*;.

ṁ (anusvara) — a resonant nasal like the *n* in the French word *bon*.

ḥ (visarga) — a final h-sound: aḥ is pronounced like *aha;* iḥ like *ihi*

The consonants are pronounced as follows:

k	— as in *k*ite	kh	— as in Ec*kh*art
g	— as in *g*ive	gh	— as in di*g-h*ard
ṅ	— as in si*ng*	c	— as in *ch*air
ch	— as in staun*ch-h*eart	j	— as in *j*oy
jh	— as in he*dgeh*og	ñ	— as in ca*ny*on
ṭ	— as in *t*ub	ṭh	— as in ligh*t-h*eart
ṇ	— as r*n*a (prepare to say the r and say *na)*.	ḍha	— as in re*d-h*ot
		ḍ	— as in *d*ove

Cerebrals are pronounced with tongue to roof of mouth, but the following dentals are pronounced with tongue against teeth:

t — as in *t*ub but with tongue against teeth.

th— as in lig*ht-h*eart but tongue against teeth.

d — as in *d*ove but tongue against teeth.

dh—as in re*d-h*ot but with tongue against teeth.

n — as in *n*ut but with tongue in between teeth.

p — as in *p*ine	ph — as in u*p-h*ill (not *f)*
b — as in *b*ird	bh — as in ru*b-h*ard
m— as in *m*other	y — as in *y*es
r — as in *r*un	l — as in *l*ight
v — as in *v*ine	s — as in *s*un

ś (palatal) as in the *s* in the German word *sprechen.*

ṣ (cerebral) — as the *sh* in shine

h — as in *h*ome

There is no strong accentuation of syllables in Sanskrit, only a flowing of short and long (twice as long as the short) syllables.

Glossary

Ācārya—One who teaches by example. The bona fide spiritual master.

Akarma or *Naiṣkarma*—Actions which free one from the cycle of birth and death.

Antaryāmi—The Lord in His plenary expansion within the heart, the Witness of all we do.

Anupaśyati—To see or observe. It is used for one who observes the Supreme Lord within everything. This means one must follow the previous *ācārya*, the perfected teacher, not to see as one does with the materially defective naked eye but by hearing from a Superior Source.

Apāpaviddham—Description of Supreme Lord—sin cannot touch Him.

Aparā—Inferior energy of the Supreme Lord. Also called *avidyā*.

Aparā Prakṛti—Inferior or material energy of the Lord; the elements of Nature are earth, fire, water, air, ether, mind, intelligence, and false ego.

Apauruṣeya—Not delivered by any person of the mundane world—words spoken by the Supreme Lord.

Arcā—The Appearance of the Supreme Lord in a Deity Form engraved from wood, stone, or other matter.

Asambhūti—Those who have no independent existence.

Asura—Those ignorant or neglectful of Kṛṣṇa conscious responsibilities.

Ātma-bhūta or *Brahmā-bhūta*—Joyful transcendental realization that one's self is not the body but spirit soul; after *ātma-bhūta* or *Brahmā-bhūta*, the next step is realizing one's loving service relationship unto the Supreme *Ātman* or Supreme *Brahman,* the Personality of Godhead.

Ātma-hana—The killer of the soul, who, for failing to use the human form of life for self-realization, must enter into the planets of darkness and ignorance.

Avidyā—Ignorance, nescience.

Avyakta—The non-manifested stage when all living beings are merged into devastating water, during the night time of Brahmā. During this time no living beings remain manifested, although spiritually they continue to exist in a dormant state.

Bhagavān—The Possessor of all opulences or all fortune, the Supreme Personality of Godhead.

Brahmā—The first living entity; as empowered by the Supreme Lord, Brahmā creates the material worlds and is their chief administrator.

Brahma-bhūta—See Atma-bhūta.

Brahman—Impersonal, unmanifest realization of the Absolute Truth. Realization of the *Brahman* aspect of the Absolute Truth is not complete unless one progresses to understand *Paramātmā* and *Bhagavān.* Understanding of *Brahman* is compared to understanding only the effulgent aspect of the Sun. One who knows not only the sunshine but also the sun globe knows more and is compared to the *yogi.* One who actually goes to the sun planet and meets the sun god knows all about the sun, sun globe, and sunshine—and he is compared to a devotee of the Personality of Godhead.

Brahmacarya—Student life according to Vedic system—

characterized by celibacy. The student is always engaged in study and devotional service under the bona fide spiritual master.

Brahmā-randhra—Highest circle of air located on top of the head. The perfect *yogi* can transfer his soul through this circle and leave the material body to take a spiritual body which never has to meet death or change.

Brahma-jyoti—Effulgence emanating from the Body of the Supreme Personality of Godhead. Perfection of realization of the Absolute Truth necessitates going beyond the glaring effulgence to perceive the Supreme Personality of Godhead as He is and to render Him eternal loving service.

Brahma-saṁhitā—Important Vedic scripture written by Lord Brahmā, the first living entity, in which are disclosed Activities of Goloka, Kṛṣṇa's Abode.

Brāhmaṇa—The learned, spiritual class, responsible for guiding all other classes for spiritual upliftment. *Brāhmaṇa* status is determined by quality, not birth.

Bhakti—Devotional service to the Supreme Lord. It is stated in *Bhagavad-gītā* that one surpasses all the stages of transcendental progressions by simple adoption of the devotional attitude; and without the injection of *bhakti*, there is no success in any transcendental process.

Buddha—Really learned. Arjuna became *buddha* by hearing the Vedic knowledge of *Bhagavad-gītā* and becoming a worshiper of the Supreme Lord, Śri Kṛṣṇa. Also, Lord Buddha, listed in the *Śrīmad-Bhāgavatam* as an incarnation of the Personality of Godhead, appearing in the beginning of *Kali-yuga* and preaching the doctrine of nonviolence to all living entities.

Complete Whole—Refers to the Personality of Godhead.

Controller—God is the Controller. The individual entities are controlling their own bodies only, but God is controlling all bodies including planetary systems, stars, moons, the cosmic manifestation, time, space and the activities of the material and spiritual energies.

Garbhodaka-śāyī Viṣṇu—An expansion from the Prime *Puruṣa Avatar*, Mahā Viṣṇu. (See *Karanodaka-śāyī Viṣṇu.) Garbhodaka-śāyī Viṣṇu* enters into each universe and lies down on the *Garbha* Ocean; from His navel a lotus stem sprouts and on this lotus Brahmā, the lord of the material universe, is born.

Gopīs—Cowherd girl friends of Kṛṣṇa in Vṛndāvana. The purest devotees of Lord Kṛṣṇa, who are unapproachable in terms of their highest standard of pure devotion for the Personality of Godhead.

Govardhana Hill—Hill in Vṛndāvana where Lord Kṛṣṇa had transcendental Pastimes with cows and cowherdsboys. The nature of Govardhana is that it is non-different from Kṛṣṇa Himself. The Absolute Truth is non-different from His Name, Fame, Land, devotees, Entourage.

Govinda—A Name for Kṛṣṇa, the Cowherd Boy, the Pleaser of the senses.

Hiraṇmaya Pātra—The dazzling covering preventing the imper-sonalists from seeing the Personality of Godhead.

Hiraṇyakaśipu—The most powerful materialist of his time.

He tried to be immortal for the sake of material enjoyment but was killed by the Claws of Lord Nṛsiṁha, the *avatāra* of Godhead in the Form of half-lion, half-man.

Iconoclasts—Those who refuse to accept that God can appear in the Form of Deities supposedly made of earth or stone. They do not accept as reality the inconceivable potencies of God, by which He, as the one Source of all energies, can convert material energy into spiritual energy according to His own will.

Iśāvāsya—God-centered. *Iśopaniṣad* instructs there is no harm in any activity such as family life or politics, provided the center of the activity is God.

Jñānins—Persons engaged in mental speculation as a means to realizing the Absolute Truth, such as philosophers and metaphysical poets. By the *jñāna* process one can reach to the realization of the Absolute Truth as *Brahman.*

Kaniṣṭha Adhikāri—A person in the lowest stage of realization of God, who worships in the temple or church according to routine formulas but who does not realize the respective advancement of different devotees or the Spiritual Nature of the Supreme Lord.

Karanodaka-śāyī Viṣṇu or *Mahā-Viṣṇu*—The gigantic expansion of the Lord Who lies down in the Causal Ocean in a section of the Spiritual Sky. Innumerable universes are generated from the pores of His body when He breathes, and they exist only during the period of His outgoing breath. All this is related in *Śrīmad-Bhāgavatam.*

Karma—Actions done in terms of prescribed duties

mentioned in scriptures. By the law of *karma* every action in the material world has a reaction, pious or impious. In *Bhagavad-gītā,* the Supreme Personality of Godhead, Śrī Kṛṣṇa, promises release from all material reaction to whomever surrenders unto Him.

Karma-bandhana-The bondage to one's material work, by which the eternal living being is forced to transmigrate within the material world.

Karma-yoga—Offering the fruit of one's work to Kṛṣṇa.

Karmis—Those engaged in activities of sense gratification and the resultant reactions. The *karmi* desires to work hard and enjoy the fruits of his labor without surrendering his all to God as the Owner and Controller of everything that be.

Kṣirodaka-śāyī Viṣṇu—The expansion of the Lord Who is residing on an island of white sand in an ocean of milk within the material universe, on a planet called *Śvetadvīpa.* He is also the Maintainer of the Universe and is in charge of the modes of goodness.

Mādhurya—The spiritual relationship of conjugal love with the Supreme Personality of Godhead, as enjoyed by the cowherd girls of Vṛndāvana. The sex attraction as known in the material world is a perverted reflection of the original spiritual relationship of *Mādhurya* existing eternally in the Spiritual World between the Lord and His conjugal Associates.

Madhyam Adhikāri—Devotees in the intermediate stage of devotional service, who save their love for the Supreme Lord, make loving friendships with devotees, teach the innocent and avoid the outright atheists.

Mahābhāgavata—Great personality who sees everything in relation to the Supreme Personality of Godhead.

Martya Loka—The place of death. Refers to the whole material world.

Material Nature—Stringent laws operating on all living beings born into the material world, by which they evolve through the species of life, suffering in the cycles of repeated births and deaths. Vedic scriptures state that the only hope of permanently quitting the material world is to surrender to Krsna, the Absolute Truth.

Māyayā apahṛta-jñāna—Class of men who think that they themselves are God, and that there is no necessity of worshiping any other God. They are unable, however, to answer how they have come under the control of the illusory energy, subject to the conditions of birth, death, disease and old age and restricted by the modes of goodness, passion and ignorance. God Himself, even when He visits this planet, is never subjected to its material laws, nor is He forced to take a body by His past actions, as are the ordinary living entities or the *māyayā apahṛta-jñāna.*

Muḍhās—Asses. The word is used in the *Bhagavad-gītā* to describe those engaged in the pursuit of sense gratification.

Nārada—The great sage who travels through the universe playing his *vīṇā* and distributing the Hare Kṛṣṇa chant. He is called the original spiritual master; many great devotees are his disciples, such as Vyāsadeva and Prahlād.

Narādhama—The lowest of human beings. Refers to those who do not use the human form of life for going back to Godhead.

Nārāyaṇa—Plenary manifestation of Lord Kṛṣṇa, thus Nārāyaṇa and Kṛṣṇa are one and the same. Nārāyaṇa existed before creation, and He created the cosmic manifestation by His self-desire.

Nirguṇa—Without attributes, without material qualifications. Is also used to mean that the Supreme Person's qualities are beyond estimation.

Paramātman (the Supersoul)—Expansion of the Supreme Lord by which He is appearing locally in the heart of all living entities, giving them memory and forgetfulness. The individual souls are *ātman.* The principal *ātman,* who controls them all, is Supersoul, *Paramātman.*

Param Brahman—The Supreme Spirit. *Param Brahman* is as much a Person as the individual living entities. As each individual is constitutionally a minute spirit soul, so He is the Supreme Soul, full in *Sac-cid-ānanda-vigraha.* Minute *Brahman* spirit souls exist for the Pleasure of *Param Brahman.*

Paramparā—Line of disciplic succession. Only from a bona fide spiritual master in the authorized, unbroken chain of disciplic succession, coming down from Kṛṣṇa, can the Vedic knowledge by realized.

Parā Prakṛti—The superior spiritual energy of the Lord—the living beings belong to the *Parā Prakṛti,* but are under the proprietary right of the Supreme Being; due to contact with material nature, the living entities' higher nature is suspended, under the influence of the material modes of goodness, passion and ignorance.

Parā Śakti—Superior energy different from this material

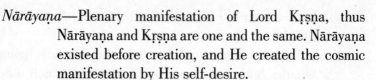

inferior Nature. Superior energy is eternal and deathless—this is the original nature of all the living entities. Also *Parā Prakṛti.*

Paribhū—Description of Godhead. The greatest of all; no one is greater than He.

Prahlād Mahārāj—The boy devotee who was saved from his demoniac father Hiraṇyakaśipu by Lord Nṛsiṁha, half-lion, half-man incarnation of Kṛṣṇa.

Prāṇa Vāyu—Movements of different kinds of air within the body. The *yogis* study to control these airs and move the soul, which is supposed to rise from one circle of air to another.

Prasādam—Mercy of God. Food offered to the Lord and distributed by the devotee as Divine remnants. In the *Bhagavad-gītā* the Lord says that He accepts fruits, vegetables, and grains from the hands of the pure devotee.

Purāṇas—Supplimentary Vedic literature. There are eighteen *Purāṇas,* intended for the gradual upliftment of the conditioned soul to spiritual life. Six *Purāṇas* are meant for the understanding of those in the modes of ignorance, six for the understanding of those in passion, and six for those in the mode of goodness—culminating in "the spotless *Purāṇa,*" *Śrīmad-Bhāgavatam,* which is the ripened fruit of all Vedic literature.

Pūrṇam—All-perfect, the Supreme Lord. There is no chance of His being subject to the laws of material Nature.

Puruṣa—Enjoyer, Male. Used for the Supreme Lord. Lord Kṛṣṇa in His original Form never leaves Vṛndāvana in the Spiritual Sky; all the affairs of His different creations are carried out by His plenary expansion or Puruṣa incarnation. The ordinary conditioned living entity tries to imitate the Puruṣa as the enjoyer of the material world, but his real eternal position is as eternal servant of the Supreme Lord.

Rāsa Dance—The sublime and spiritual Pastime of the Supreme Lord with the *gopīs,* conducted on the exchange of conjugal love without any of the inebrieties of lust as found in the material world. *Rāsa* dance has to be understood from the lips of a pure devotee of Kṛṣṇa.

Ṛsis—Philosophers, mystics. Used generally for those thinkers who try to reach the Absolute by their tiny brain power. They can reach only negative definitions of the Absolute. The Absolute Truth, Personality of Godhead, is revealed only to the devotee engaged in transcendental devotional service.

Rudra—Lord Śiva, controller of the material modes of ignorance; at the time of dissolution of the material worlds, Śiva is in charge of destruction.

Saguṇa—With qualities. The worship of the Supreme Lord with attributes, as in worship of the Deity in the temple, does not mean that the Lord comes under the laws of material nature, although He has qualities and appears in the material form (wood, stone, etc.). For Him there is no difference between material and spiritual energies, as He is the Source and Controller of both.

Sākhya—Relationship of friendship with the Supreme Lord. Arjuna had this relationship.

Sambhūti—The Absolute Personality of Godhead Who is absolutely independent.

Sambhavat—Worship of the Supreme Cause.

Sannyāsa—Renounced order of life. *Sannyāsa* does not mean to go off to the jungle and renounce all activity, but to surrender everything to Kṛṣṇa. Even a householder or married man living in the world can do this, under the instructions of a bona fide spiritual master.

Sac-cid-ānanda-vigraha—Eternal, knowing and blissful—in full form. Both the Supreme Personality of Godhead and the living entities share this nature; but His nature is infinite, and His parts and parcels are infinitesimal.

Śaṅkara—Impersonalist *ācārya* who taught supremacy of *Brahma-jyoti*, the effulgence emanating from the Body of the Supreme Lord. Although he does not belong to the personalist cult, Śaṅkara has admitted that Nārāyaṇa and Kṛṣṇa are one and that Nārāyaṇa is the Supreme Personality of Godhead, transcendental to the material modes.

Śānta—The spiritual relationship of calmness or the neutral relationship between the Supreme Lord and His loving associates, as had by the four Kumāra sages who were always in meditation on the greatness of God.

Sense enjoyment—Illusory life of trying to enjoy with the body, without surrendering to the Complete Whole.

Srīla Bhaktivinode Thākur—Great *Ācārya* in disciplic succession from Lord Caitanya, pioneer of Kṛṣṇa Consciousness in the modern age. Father of Bhakti Siddhānta Sarasvatī, the spiritual master of A.C. Bhaktivedānta Swāmī.

Śrīmatam—A Vaiśya, member of mercantile community.

Śuci—A spiritually advanced *Brāhmaṇa*.

Śuddham—Most purified. Descriptive Name of Supreme Lord.

Śukadeva Gosvāmī— The great spiritual master who related the *Śrīmad-Bhāgavatam* for the first time to Mahārāj Parīkṣit. He is the son of Vyāsadeva.

Sura—Godly. One who knows and carries out the responsibility of God-consciousness.

Tri-pāda-vibhūti—The Spiritual Nature beyond the jurisdiction of Brahmā—the superior energy of the Lord. Also called *Parā Prakṛti.*

Vaikuṇṭha-lokas—Spiritual planets situated in the spiritual sky; planetary Abodes of the Supreme Personality of Godhead. The only places of permanence, without any anxieties.

Vātsālya—Relationship of paternal affection with the Supreme Lord, as had by Nanda and Yaśodā, who enjoyed the Childhood Pastimes of Kṛṣṇa as His father and mother in Vṛndāvana.

Veda-vāda-ratā—Those who study the *Vedas* for attaining results such as heaven. Also called *Vidyārata* they are condemned by *Īśopaniṣad* for studying the *Vedas* in an unauthorized way, without knowing the goal of the *Vedas,* the Personality of Godhead.

Vedic knowledge—Transcendental knowledge spoken by the Supreme Lord and compiled in scripture; perfect knowledge coming down through unbroken disciplic succession.

Vidyā—Knowledge.

Vikarma—Actions done in misuse of one's freedom, or prohibitive acts, which direct oneself to the lower regions of life.

Vināśa—Temporary material manifestation.

Virāṭa Form—The Universal Form of God. This Form is mainly for the neophyte who cannot understand Kṛṣṇa as the Supreme Spiritual Entity. The *Virāṭa* Form is composed of the entire material ingredients of the Universe, seen as the body of the Lord—but it is not His eternal Form.

Viṣṇu-tattva—A plenary portion of the Supreme Lord, Śrī Kṛṣṇa. These expansions are the same in potency, but Kṛṣṇa is the original Personality of Godhead. For example, many candles may be lit from one candle and the candles are equal in illumination to the original, but they are still not the original. The Original Personality of Godhead, the Source of all *Viṣṇu-tattvas* is Śrī Kṛṣṇa.

Vṛndāvana—Place in India where Lord Kṛṣṇa displayed His eternal, transcendental Pastimes 5,000 years ago. Vṛndāvana is also the name of Kṛṣṇa's Abode in the topmost spiritual planet, Goloka. The pure devotee is able to see the Vṛndāvana within this material world as non-different from Vṛndāvana in the spiritual sky. His Land, Vṛndāvana, is non-different from Himself.

Vyāsadeva—The literary incarnation of Kṛṣṇa who compiled all the Vedic literatures.

Yogis—Those who practice the *yoga* process (linking with the Supreme). The purpose of the *Haṭha* and *Aṣṭāṅga-yoga* systems, i.e., sitting postures, breath control, meditation, is to control the senses and see the Form of the Personality of Godhead within the heart.

Yoga-bhraṣṭas—Souls fallen from the path of self realization.

INDEX

INDEX

INDEX

INDEX